A. S. Hale

Henderson, N.C.

Messenger 88 yrs. of age
"I can't do much, I can't say much
but I can show which side I'm on"

BOOKS BY ALBERT EDWARD DAY

JESUS AND HUMAN PERSONALITY
PRESENT PERILS IN RELIGION
REVITALIZING RELIGION

Jesus and Human Personality

ALBERT EDWARD DAY

THE ABINGDON PRESS
NEW YORK CINCINNATI CHICAGO

DAY
JESUS AND HUMAN PERSONALITY

Printed in the United States of America

CONTENTS

FOREWORD

THIS book contains the Lectures given under the auspices of the Lyman Beecher Foundation at Yale University in April, 1934. Chapter I has been added in order that those who were not permitted to share the fellowship of Convocation Week might have a better understanding of the spirit and purpose of this series. These lectures were delivered extemporaneously and as soon after as possible were reduced to manuscript. Earnest endeavor has been made to retain the style as well as the substance of the spoken word.

This year's Lecturer wishes to express to the Faculty and students of Yale Divinity School his deep appreciation of the bountiful courtesies extended to him during this eventful week, and especially for the thoughtful and enthusiastic reception given to his efforts to interpret the ministry of Jesus to the making of human personality. The week at Yale will remain one of life's most splendid memories and a constant inspiration to a more life-giving ministry.

Gratitude is due my efficient secretary, Miss Catherine Logan, not only for her assistance in preparation of the manuscript for the press but for invaluable suggestions as to the plan and content of the lectures and for many constructive criticisms as to their final form.

ALBERT EDWARD DAY.

CHAPTER I

PREACHING AND PERSONALITY

ONE of my distinguished predecessors in this Lectureship gave a most stimulating series on *The Art of Preaching*. That is exactly what preaching is—an art! It can never become a science with fixed formulas, obedience to which will assure uniform results. Once having ascertained the chemical content of water and the conditions under which hydrogen and oxygen unite, the scientist can enter his laboratory in the confidence that ere he emerges, water will have been produced by the creation of prescribed conditions and the observance of familiar rules. But the preacher cannot be so sure that on any day the water of life will be provided for his thirsting congregations. He approaches each sermon more as the artist comes to a new canvas. The painter has conceptions of reality or feelings about it, struggling for expression. But he is not certain that he will be able to give these ideas and emotions convincing interpretation through the medium of color and line. Nor can he be confident that the public will catch his ideas or share his emotions. When the painting—any painting—is finished, the artist may feel that there is much that he tried to symbolize by his paints which still remains vague and formless and haunting in his own mind; or that what did achieve some clarity of conception escaped the language of the brush; or that as far as his original conviction is concerned, the public remains in ignorance and he himself is still a solitary soul. Ever and anon, however, when the final touch has been given to his canvas, the artist knows that something eternal has come to birth in his own eager mind, has succeeded in working its way through his trained fingers and in embodying itself in tints and figures whose significance anyone with æsthetic hunger and training must appreciate. In that hour he knows the supreme rapture of the experience of an effectively shared vision of reality.

That is the experience of the preacher too. If he cares for people and is eager to lead them into a new understanding and appreciation of saving reality, he will find, as he broods over their problems, ideas and emotions struggling for expression. But he cannot be sure that adequate expression will be found before eleven o'clock on any Sunday morning. He may toil faithfully and pray earnestly. He may labor with his pen as diligently as the artist does with his brush, in an effort to clarify his ideas and identify his deep emotions. He may summon all the technique of public speech to his assistance when he mounts his pulpit and endeavors to give his sermon convincing utterance. But after it is all over he may go down to his house unjustified, aware that he has failed, haunted with visions too elusive as yet to be captured in speech, or crushed by the consciousness that what lay in the alembic of his own mind clear and convincing, somehow failed to make an appeal and to awaken an affirmation and appreciation in the minds of his hearers. Every preacher knows the bitterness of this experience —to have sermons which fail to arrive in the study though one has sweat blood in the effort to summon them from the deep of his own dim awareness that there is something there which ought to be said. Every preacher knows too the pang of facing a congregation with something which an hour before was to his own heart a living, fascinating characterization of reality, and then of having that creation disintegrate under influences emanating from his congregation, leaving him with halting mind and a horrified heart, aware that what he is and believes and has felt are neither understood nor appreciated. The most brilliant do not escape such frustrations. There are five preachers in America whom every competent judge would rank among our dozen best. Of one of them an enthusiastic but discriminating hearer said, "His preaching is awfully thin sometimes." Another preached before a university audience a sermon which made them wish ere the sermon was done that some good angel might descend and leave something for them to carry home. They were receiving no gift from the man who stood in the pulpit. Another appeared at a church celebration preceded by great anticipations. He is one of the most uniformly successful preachers in his denomination. His perfection has long been the envy of many who still groan and travail in pain, waiting for their homiletic redemption. But on that great occasion Apollos floundered heavily in the mire for a half hour and then stuck. Not all the king's horses nor all the king's men could have saved him or his sermon that day. The fourth is as true a prophet of God as the American pulpit boasts. He came to a gathering of preachers with what he hoped would be a masterpiece. But as the hour proceeded he knew and all the spectators knew that his sermonic brush had merely daubed another canvas. Failure was not the result of lack of toil nor of sturdy Christian manhood but of those imponderables which distinguish an art from a science.

There is something almost eerie about the work of preaching. A man may come to his hour with thorough preparation and the confidence of discovered and wrought-out truth and yet fail. He may be summoned in an emergency to speak with little or no preparation and achieve a triumph.

A Methodist Chrysostom visited a city in Indiana with a famous lecture which he had delivered hundreds of times with pathos and power to audiences east and west. But something went wrong that night. After an apparently normal beginning, the audience became aware that it was not interested. But it listened on in confidence that soon the inevitable interest would be aroused—for the lecturer had a charm which was usually irresistible. That confidence was without foundation, for after forty minutes the two-hour lecture had disintegrated until the lecturer himself would have no more to do with it. He closed abruptly and left the stage. He had not forgotten his lines. He was not sick. But his gift had failed him. Why, he did not know. Nor is it likely that any investigation would have revealed the secret. For preaching is not a science but an art and is subject to all the variations that distinguish the studio from the laboratory.

The life of the preacher would be intolerable if the artist's frustration did not alternate with the artist's fulfillment. But it does, thank God. There are times when what was first a mere hint, a timid visitor knocking at the door of the mind, a feeling of uneasiness or longing, becomes a clear conception, crossing the threshold and taking such complete possession that one's whole mental life is reintegrated about a new center; times when one knows and knows that he knows and when that knowledge is aflame with a passion which enkindles a like flame in one's audience; times when speaker and listener are caught up together in an absorbing unity of thought and feeling, of conviction and aspiration, and even adoration, which makes the quiet of the benediction seem like the cessation of a great symphony; times when the people enter into the mood of Peter at the transfiguration, "Let us make three tabernacles here," and are loathe to depart; times when the preacher escapes the isolation of his own soul and shares the ineffable rapture of communion with the souls of his own people through a masterpiece whose production he cannot wholly explain but whose birth is payment for the sweat and toil of years.

To be sure, even an art has technique which must be mastered—the laws of color combination, of perspective, of symmetry, the skill to draw a tree that will look like a tree and not a mere blur upon the landscape, to paint men that will look not like trees walking or mere "forked animals," but men. To some moderns such technique is taboo and the result has been devastating. One picture at the International Art Exhibit in Pittsburgh hung upside down for weeks before even the judges discovered its plight. The scorn of technique which characterizes some artists has produced pictures which might as well hang upside down or even diagonally. The spectator could not possibly have any more difficulty in recognizing the contents of the canvas than he does when the hanging is as the artist intended. But such artistic insanity cannot long endure. The pictures it has painted will some day hang in museums along with samples of the writings of Gertrude Stein as an evidence of the madness of our time, and people will turn again to admire pictures by those artists who have been at pains to master technique.

Preaching too has its technique, and it is very important. Absence of it has created sermons whose lack of logic, violation of rhetoric, abuse of words, distraction of illustration, have been so confusing that it would not have made very much difference whether the sermon were repeated backward or forward. The people who came to pray went away to scoff or to mourn. Irritation and bewilderment were the preacher's only achievement. "Mother," a little girl whispered, as she watched the mounting frenzy in the pulpit, "the preacher is getting mad, isn't he?" About all that even adults frequently get from some preaching is a surmise that the preacher is terribly angry about something or ecstatically pleased about something else, but there is little direction offered to their own wrath and little inspiration to their own gladness. Not often is the situation so hopeless as that, but one is sure that the ministry of many a man would be greatly increased in effectiveness if he observed with greater care some of the simple rules of homiletics. Technique is as important in the study as in the studio.

Important too is the technique of the platform. Whether one shall preach with or without notes, whether he shall memorize or speak extemporaneously, whether he shall employ any of the arts of the actor or shall carry on a quiet conversation before an audience, the use of voice and gesture—all of these matters merit careful consideration. Frequently young preachers are absorbed in them to the exclusion of other questions relating to the preacher's task. Every successful preacher knows what an advantage effective delivery gives to the truth. The most sublime conceptions in the preacher's mind often make little impression on his congregation because they have been so carelessly phrased and so feebly uttered. The simplest truths are worthy of noblest expression. So cluttered are the minds of the average crowd with false notions that only the realities which are given forceful utterance can make an entrance and find a place for themselves.

But art is not all technique. It is also content. Not even the skill of a Rembrandt or a Raphael can give significance to trivial subject matter or make true what is false or bestow permanence on what is only transitory. More fundamental in the art of preaching than the question "how to preach" is that other issue, "What shall I preach?" The preacher is supremely the artist of reality. He paints for a purpose. He is not free to follow his own fancy, to use his pulpit for the exploitation of his own genius or for the advertisement of his own pet reactions to life. He is summoned to a specific kind of discovery and to a definite task of interpretation.

The one who accepts an invitation to so important a mission as is prescribed by the Lyman Beecher Foundation may choose between lectures on the technique or on the content of preaching. It seemed to the one on whose unworthy shoulders the responsibility has fallen this year that his imperious summons was to present as clearly and as faithfully as he could some convictions as to the content of the preacher's message to this age of confusion. Particularly did he feel called to ask once again what contribution preaching can be to the making of human personality. In the effort to suggest an answer he has read widely and has levied upon his years of experience in attempting to meet the needs and solve the problems of individuals who have come to his study for help, or have summoned him to their homes and offices, or have attended his ministry with faces which have told their own tragic story of hunger and defeat.

This momentous undertaking has brought me face to face with two difficult questions—"What is the nature of personality?" "Have we in Jesus an answer to the demands of personality?" In seeking truth about these problems, anyone will find himself immediately thrust into the arena of hot debate, where it is vain to hope for agreement among experts, or for final conclusions. My own tendency more than once was to retreat from the field and turn in the direction where one might hope to lie down in green pastures and beside the still waters. But such a retreat was impossible. It would have taken me away from my own task and would have been a surrender of the most important responsibilities of my ministry. It too would have been a refusal to share with my brethren my own experience in the partial fulfillment of those responsibilities. I had had some success in dealing with problems of personality. And I had found Jesus to be the central influence in that success. I could not refuse, therefore, to bring to others whatever light had come to me in my studies and in my clinic of life.

That, in substance, is what these lectures are. They make no pretense of a final answer to all the questions which must come to the intelligent mind confronted either by the historic Jesus or by the sick souls of a parish. They are simply the humble offering of values by one who has cared greatly for his people and has found in Jesus the Master light of all his seeing and seeks always to keep close to reality.

New light is constantly arriving on problems of personality. I have tried not to become entangled either in the jargon of schools of psychology or in hypotheses which to-morrow may prove utterly inadequate. Historical research is still occupied with Jesus and may have still greater wisdom for us who are eager to know more about this winsome, wonderful Man. But both in psychology and history some results have been achieved, some conclusions established which are very fruitful in the clarification of the needs of personality and in the provision of an answer. They have been tried and not found wanting. Some of these results have found their way into these lectures and are submitted not as tentative guesses but as discovered goods.

In brief, the method employed has been to make as clear as possible the problems of personality and then their answer in Jesus. It may seem to some that an undue space has been given to problems and not enough to answers. The reasons have been two: first, that perhaps the greatest need of the ministry is to become aware of the problems of personality—too many seem to be almost wholly unaware of either the perplexity or the poignancy of those problems—they need to become problem-conscious; second, because once the problems are clearly seen, the answer in Jesus, while never simple nor facile, can be briefly presented. It remains and must always remain for the individual preacher to work out the manifold applications of that answer to his own preaching.

CHAPTER II

PERSONALITY AND SOCIETY

JESUS was supremely concerned with personality. He shocked the religious leaders of his day by his insistence that the institution should always be subordinate to the individual. "The Sabbath was made for man, not man for the Sabbath." He outraged their sense of social and religious propriety by keeping company with sinners big and little, and the only defense he offered was that his chief calling was to be a physician of broken personality. "Wilt thou be made whole?" he is reported to have asked of a man whose poor, palsied body lay upon a stretcher before him. But that was not the only time he raised that question with anybody. As he walked up and down the streets and roads of Galilee and went in and out of the homes and synagogues and market places, meeting people in daytime crowds or in midnight solitudes, his eager eyes, quick to perceive the wounds which life had inflicted upon them, seemed always to be asking, "Wilt thou be made whole? Do you not want to recover your lost integrity? Do you not want to achieve unity and peace and power?" The complaint most often urged against Jesus is that he seemed to have no interest in social reform. He lived in a slave-owning world, but as far as we know made no argument in behalf of emancipation. His people were exploited by Roman imperialism, but apparently he only urged them to submit gracefully. There was a yawning gulf between rich and poor, but he offered no political devices for the redistribution of wealth. False conclusions have been drawn from his silences and his inaction, both by those who believe in him and those who repudiate his moral and religious leadership, but even these false conclusions are a revelation of the inescapable premise, namely, that the mission of Jesus was, to use the catch word of modern religious education, personality-centered. He wanted above all things to make men and women who should be persons fit for a place in the kingdom of persons; who should be children of the supreme Person, living the fullness of life which characterizes true sons of God.

What is our attitude toward personality? This question has been submerged in many pulpits and churches beneath the rising tides of interest in the achievement of a new social order. More sermons are being preached, more books written, more editorials in religious journals penned in the indictment of social sins and in pleas for social regeneration than at any other period in Christian history. A professor in one of our largest American universities was talking about one of our most brilliant preachers. His criticism was not captious but it was arresting. He said: "The doctor is a great preacher, but he is always bringing some social problem into the pulpit. He seems to forget that we have personal problems to solve, that we ourselves are problems. I wish he would quit trying to reform everything and would sometime see what he could do for me." I do not think the situation was quite as bad as that threnody of despair seemed to indicate, but I do think that that professorial wail is a reminder of what has been taking place in many churches in America. There has been a change of mood—from a quest for souls to a quarrel with systems, political, industrial, commercial. There has been a change in method—from an effort to transform individuals to a crusade for the reformation of society. There has been a reinterpretation of morals so that the old concern about the familiar devil's trinity, drunkenness, lust, and gambling, has been replaced by agitation over unregulated individualism, social coercion, class strife, nationalism, and war. There has been a shift in religious emphasis, from the surrender which will make one right with God to a sacrificial co-operation which will make him right with the last man or woman or child affected by his conduct. There has been a change in confidence, from a God who worketh in man to will and to do of his good pleasure to laws and institutions which will make men social assets, whether it pleases them to be or not. There has even been a change in problems, from the tensions set up within the individual ("Now rest, my long divided heart") to those tensions arising within the church in the present social order, a church summoned to a social reconstruction which some think can be achieved only by violence, and at the same time committed to a gospel of love with which violence is incompatible.

This change has no doubt been accentuated by current events. In the past four years the blindest among us have been compelled to see that something was tragically wrong with our social organization and that a real race is on between civilization and chaos. In recent months our adventurous President has been leading the nation in an experiment to save civilization; and churchmen have had a growing conviction that such an experiment represents both a challenge and an opportunity to the church to assume its almost forfeited leadership in society. As the life of Jesus is being rewritten, he is being portrayed as chiefly concerned with saving his own nation from impending disaster, a discovery which has seemed to give his followers a new charter and summons to social action. A crusading Christ demands a crusading church.

I

That the socialization of religious passion and purpose has had its value few of us would care even to raise a question, much less enter a denial. It was inevitable for those whose hearts were made sensitive by spiritual fellowship with Jesus. It is impossible for some of us to understand how there could be indifference or inaction in the presence of the contemporary social scene: enormous profits for the few accumulated at the expense of a living wage for many; heartless speculation with the savings of honest toil; luxuriant idleness supported by the sweat and weariness of those who know neither comfort nor freedom from care; exploitation both of human need and human passion by panderers to sex and purveyors of worthless drugs and unclean foods; all the human wastage of preventable poverty, and all the human wretchedness involved in the fear of it, and all the human debauchery by drugs and drink in the effort to find a little escape from its misery; the denial of culture, the destruction of opportunity for a truly moral life; the poisoning of life's springs by the bitterness of competition for a job or for customers; the pitiless discrimination against men and women because of the pigment of their skin or the practice of their religion; the destruction of property and life and the collapse of civilization because nations have not found a better way to settle disputes than the arbitrament of gun powder and poison gas. It is all such a devil's caldron, brewed in a hell of ignorance and selfishness, that anyone who has any interest in humanity must want to upset the caldron and exterminate the brewers, making an end of the system which gave it a place, and if possible so to reconstruct political and economic life that there will be no more room for such a witch's device than there is for the potations and incantations of medicine men in a scientific laboratory.

Let it be understood now that this writer is entirely in sympathy with the fight for social redemption. Awakened from his dream of individualistic religion by the prophetic pages of Rauschenbusch, he soon found himself flung into the arena of social conflict and felt the blows which intrenched privilege understands so well how to inflict upon anyone who questions its polite plunder and seeks to dislodge it from the power and wealth which is its stronghold. He has known the rapture and also the terrors of battle. In steel strike and coal strike and taxicab strike it has been his privilege to plead for justice and to espouse the cause of those who were no longer able to defend their rights. Before city councils and legislatures and governors he has gone to lift a voice for human welfare and to plead, "Let my people go." He has faced some of the most unscrupulous exploiters of their fellow men in America and has listened to threats whose execution would have meant one less minister in the community. Nor does he anticipate any retreat from this battle line where he has stood during these years in the name of Christ and humanity. If he thought the church would give him no license to unsheathe his homiletic sword against these foes of human welfare, he would resign from his pulpit and hire a hall, or, lacking funds to do that, he would claim the American privilege of a soap box and, standing under the canopy of God's free sky, with only the noises of the street for his choir, would speak in behalf of those social reforms whose crying need must be apparent to any truly Christian intelligence. He does not in the least degree share the views of those who placidly announce that the social gospel is a modern invention which has no relation to the essentials of Christianity and who piously declare that the preacher's business is with individuals and not with institutions, and who unctuously proclaim that if we lead men to God, he will tell them what to do without any assistance from us, and that thus social life will be reconstructed as far as and as fast as there is enough of the grace of God in men's hearts to inspire such transformation. This preacher believes that it is his business to help create a social conscience and to suggest to that conscience objectives near and remote which, if realized, will make this world the scene, not of a dying social system which "commits the hypocrisy of hiding its injustices behind the forms of justice" but of a flexible social organism which will provide for the health, moral growth, and spiritual nurture of all, regardless of race or class.

Nor is there in this heart any sympathy with the position of the Barthians, who are succeeding in attracting a great deal of attention by their challenge to everything and everybody which hitherto have passed for Christian. Barth himself is so hopeless about man, and conceives him to be so utterly fallen from his estate as creature and son of God, that he is sure that "our criticizing, protesting, reforming, organizing, democratizing, socializing, revolutionizing—however fundamental and thoroughgoing these may be—will not satisfy the kingdom of God";[1] that we cannot seriously use "the thought forms of Jesus as the law for every economic, racial, national, and international order"; that all our efforts to Christianize society really only "furnish it with an ecclesiastical cupola or wing";[2] and that the Christian in society "can but follow attentively what is done by God."[3] Barth's associate, Brunner, declares that the social gospel has brought the gospel of Jesus into disrepute; that if the church followed it, "it would in two generations, or perhaps sooner, be reduced to a protesting rump of visionary fanatics," and that "the social and political world is much too far off from God really to be moved by protests, social programs, principles, and ideals."[4] Such despair of human nature, its dreams, its hopes, its purposes, its possibilities; such separation of man from God that man's best is not even a shadow of God's will; such renunciation of responsibility for right social action as to transfer the whole task to the shoulders of the Almighty, seem to me to be both irrational and unchristian. They ascribe to us the paradox of a knowledge great enough to know that our politics and economics are wrong but not great enough even to begin to understand what might be done to make them right. And they leave man a marionette in the grip of God, man's only wisdom being recognition of his own utter helplessness and resignation to the movements of the Unseen Hand.

II

But having said all that, and having affirmed an interest in social reconstruction, and having made a dedication to loyal and sacrificial labor in its behalf, nevertheless it must be affirmed because it needs to be affirmed once again that personality is and must be our chief concern. We want a better social order not for the sake of the order but for the sake of people. Sometimes in agitation and argument that palpable fact is forgotten and agitators and apologists miss the corrective influence which a consideration of personality would exercise over their schemes and strategies. A mother with a passion for cleanliness and sartorial splendor washed her boy until he was spotless, combed and brushed his hair until every strand was in place, dressed him in white, starched linen, and took him to a picnic. Having ensconced herself comfortably among middle-aged matrons she permitted him to wander off in the direction where the laughter of happy children seemed to indicate that somebody was having a good time, but with a solemn injunction that he was not to get "mussed up" or dirty. About the middle of the afternoon, still spick and span, but anxious and unhappy and weary-eyed, he came to his mother with a timid but pitiful plea, "Mother, may I sit down?" One more than half suspects that some reformers are more concerned in dressing up society in their own starched ideas and in imposing abstract notions of social justice, than they are in giving anybody a picnic or in releasing personality for free and happy and creative activity. Social schemes are evolved which take only partial account of human nature, providing for bread but not for the satisfactions of private property, for the opportunity to labor but not for real liberty, for social fellowship but not for fertilizing solitude, for culture but not for contacts with the Infinite. If such schemes were adopted, we might be better off, as far as our bodily needs are concerned, but we should be worse off for an answer to the demands of our whole personality. We should not be more, and we might be less truly men and women. It is not so important that life be made easier; it is important that it have an opportunity to become great. Security is something we all crave, but it would be little less than a calamity if from us were removed all demand to live dangerously. A form of social insurance which lessened the stimulus to individual initiative; government pensions which curtailed the necessity of private prudence; a planned economy which made no place for the thrust of economic genius, would not provide the environment in which personality would have its largest chance. Unless we know what the self needs for its fulfillment in personality and unless we keep the interests of such personality in the supreme place in our thinking, we shall go blundering on till the end of time, changing laws and institutions without materially improving them, altering the forms of human society but not greatly enriching human life.

Such a result might not perturb some people. Their interest in social reform is quite like that of some mechanics in a machine—if it represents an idea and runs smoothly, they are not concerned whether it has any human use or not. Their social experiments are carried on in the same spirit which takes men to arctic and antarctic regions—the satisfaction of curiosity about the unknown, unwillingness to leave any area unexplored, whether there shall be any real increment of life or not. But you and I surely do not belong to that group. We are out to help people, to help them become more truly themselves, to achieve the possibilities latent in their human inheritance, really to be persons living in fellowship with other persons and with the Person. Therefore our social crusade must be carried on in the light of the most complete understanding of personality and its needs that is available. Personality is our objective, and, like every other objective, it must be clearly understood and persistently kept in mind if it is ultimately to be attained. It must inspire all our hypotheses, inform all our procedures, sit in judgment on all our results. Society ought to be made for man and not man for society. Men are not mere political units out of which to build a state: the state ought to be an environment for the building of men. The totalitarian state is a blasphemy against manhood. So is every social scheme, communist, fascist, Republican, Democrat, which makes of itself the end. "Of the people, by the people, for the people" is the only tenable philosophy of social action. There may be times when the government ought not to be of the people's immediate will. There may be occasions for dictators and oligarchies; "of the people, by the people" may justifiably in time of stress be in suspense. But "for the people" is the universal obligation of every social system every moment of its existence. Industry must make individuals, politics persons, society souls.

III

Here we encounter one of the arresting paradoxes of life. A social order is judged by the kind of persons it produces, but at the same time a satisfying social order cannot be created without the right kind of persons. "An institution," said Emerson, "is the lengthened shadow of a man." If industry ought to make individuals, individuals do make the industry. If politics ought to open the door to personality, it is certain that personalities do determine what doors are open and shut in the realm of politics. If society should create souls, souls do give to society its form and spirit. A few men sitting at Washington may write laws and evolve codes, but whether social action in conformity with those laws and codes shall follow depends entirely upon the character of the citizenship, their ideals, their capacity for self-discipline. At the close of the Great War, while the nation's emotions were still strung to a high pitch, the Eighteenth Amendment was written into the Constitution, laws were enacted in harmony with that amendment, a vast machinery of enforcement was installed. But effective Prohibition did not arrive, because it was not in the hearts of the officials and of the people. Many men and women still wanted the stimulus of alcohol, and many other men and women thought they ought to have it if they wanted it, and many others were quite willing to run the risk and reap the reward of supplying it. And so we had bootlegging and rum-running, the bribery of officials and the debauchery of youth. Laws cannot insure a sober society; only a widespread conviction about the industrial and social menace of alcohol can do that. Mr. Roosevelt is attempting to reform business in America, to eliminate cut-throat competition, and to compel fair play between manufacturers big and little, between dealers great and small, between employers and employees. Elaborate codes have been written which embody an encouraging amount of social idealism. But we are discovering that codes are utterly dependent on the character of men affected by them. There is always a way around if men do not choose to obey. A story is going about which gives the clue to the real situation confronting us. A man went to buy a car. In the purchase he wanted to trade in his old car. The dealer named the allowance he would give for the old car but the prospective purchaser wanted a hundred dollars more. The dealer replied that the N.R.A. had established a price and he dared not go beyond it. And he did not. But he did lay a simple wager with the purchaser involving just a hundred dollars, a wager which the purchaser could not help but win. So the deal was consummated, the N.R.A. was outwitted, the dealer made a sale by giving the purchaser one hundred dollars not contemplated in the code, the attempt to secure equity among dealers was defeated, the spirit of the whole experiment was violated. The assault was one which no law could reach and no penalty prevent. Farmers were given a bonus for plowing under cotton and withdrawing the cotton acreage from cultivation. They withdrew their poorest acres and cultivated others of greater fertility, with the result that we were threatened with a greater cotton crop than before. Wages have been advanced but prices have been raised to such an extent that the purchasing power of the wage-earner is no greater than it was. Many people have said that they would not like to be in the President's shoes; such possibilities of weal and woe have descended upon him. What they ought to be saying is that they would not like to be in the shoes of the average citizen of America. Upon us, not upon him, rests responsibility for our social destiny. The wisest plan emanating from Washington can be defeated at our own firesides and in our shops and offices. The new era which he proposes can come only if there are enough new people with new outlooks, new ideals, new consecrations to "ring out the old, ring in the new." Russia found that her greatest problem is not with social mechanics but with human nature. According to Maurice Hindus, before the Marxian dream of a religionless, classless society could be realized there had to be a population from whose hearts religion, race consciousness, sex consciousness, acquisitiveness, and family passion had been eliminated. Deliberately the leaders of communism set out to alter personality. With a skill to which nothing is comparable in history they have achieved triumph after triumph, have fashioned a wholly new man, with a wholly new outlook upon the world and his own position in it. For good or ill the new man has lost all faith in God and all fear of God, all fear of sex, all fear of money, the old fear of the family, the old fear of insecurity, and he stands forth a highly regimented individual with an aim, a mission, a mentality all his own.[5] We do not like the type, but the type is necessary to a Marxian society, and it is to the credit of the communists that they have recognized it. When will American society and American churches show as great wisdom? If we are going to have a social order run for service, we must have a service-minded people who care more for people than for profits, more for personality than for power, who regard a benevolent social plan not as something to be outwitted but as a valuable instrument placed in their hands, making possible the realization in practice of the brotherhood which is in their hearts; who will be not bootleggers of wealth, racketeers of revenue, pirates of power, but citizens of the kingdom of God.

While we want a new world for the sake of new people, we must have new people for the sake of a new world. Professor Groves, defining sociology as the science that especially attempts to further human progress, makes this significant statement: "Sociology has found from experience that it can make headway . . . only as it has a better understanding of human conduct." "Thus it has been forced to dig down into individual conduct in its search for an explanation of the social experiences of men and women . . . (to draw) heavily upon psychology and psychiatry."[6] Progress is not inevitable—we have seen that will-o'-the-wisp vanish out of the swamps of human thinking. Progress depends on personality.

Sociology knows that, and the church ought to know it. Long ago Jesus, who is forever surprising us by his contemporaneousness, said, "A good tree cannot bring forth evil fruit, neither can a corrupt tree good fruit." "Do men gather grapes of thorns, or figs of thistles?" For a while we have been under the delusion that good fruit could be had in some other way, that we could agitate and legislate and, lo, grapes would appear on Maryland thorn bushes and figs on Connecticut thistles. But ever and anon sanity returns, and we discover that Jesus was right and that if we want the grapes of good will and the figs of concord and all the other fruits which social welfare demands, we must grow vines and trees of sturdy personalities rather than scrubby bushes and noxious weeds.

IV

But even our sanity has not been as clear-headed as it ought to be. We have recognized the demand for personality. But we have been too naïve in our recognition. We have not sensed the complexity of the problem involved. We have approached it with limited concepts of what may be wrong with personality and what is needed to make personality right. We have classified men as good or bad. The bad men were those who used lurid language and had ungovernable tempers and drank to excess and were careless of the property rights of others and violated virtue and, especially, did not come to church to hear us preach. The good men were those whose words the recording angel could write down without a blush, whose temper never escaped the cage of discretion, who always turned their glasses down at banquets and observed legal distinctions as to property rights and respected womanhood and sat under our sermons, sometimes awake and sometimes asleep, but at least helping to fill the empty pews. Our task, therefore, was to convince the bad of their badness when they were bad, persuade them to quit their meanness and become like those who were corraled in our churches and whom we called good. Lines were sharply and easily drawn between those who were right and those who were wrong. What made men wrong was ignorance or perversity, and what was needed to make them right was knowledge to cure their ignorance and persuasion to master their perversity.

Religious education appeared on the scene and pushed the problem and its solution farther back into the years of childhood and youth. It said, "Better build a fence at the top of the cliff than a hospital at the bottom." "As the twig is bent the tree inclines." "Give a child the right kind of culture and you will not need to convert him." For its discoveries and disciplines there is every reason to be grateful. The protest it made against the waste of youth's precious heritage; the disclaimer it entered against the notion that one could be so much better a son of God if he had played with the devil a while; the sense of responsibility it brought to parents and to the church for the creation of Christian character; the assistance it has given in the provision of curricula and the development of methods for the discharge of that responsibility, have put the ministry and the church under a debt which has often been too grudgingly acknowledged. But for a long time the educators, like the preachers, were under the tyranny of too simple a conception of personality, its problems and its possibilities and its true fulfillment in a thoroughly social ethic.

Some of us believe that of all the new ideas which are clamoring for attention at this hour none have greater significance for religion than the revised conception of personality which is knocking at our doors. It is especially a fortunate coincidence or a Divine Providence which has accompanied our ever-deepening concern for a more just, humane, life-giving social order with the beginning of an understanding of the tangled personalities which stand in the way of the realization of such an order. I say the beginning of an understanding. I think no one would pretend that we have made more than a beginning. I proposed a very simple human problem to a distinguished group of psychologists and psychiatrists not long ago. Some attempts at a solution were offered but at the end one of them said, "The question proposed is very important, but we psychiatrists will have to confess that we do not know where we are going in relation to it." And no one raised a voice in dissent. Psychoanalysts and psychiatrists and objective psychologists and neurologists differ widely among themselves in their philosophy of personality and their practical treatment of it. Inevitably one who can claim scarcely more than the position of an interested layman has no pretense of a final word. But at least enough has been discovered to make us very sure that in our effort to create good persons—that is, thoroughly social persons—who shall be fit for membership in that beloved community which we hope shall rise out of the ashes of a competitive, acquisitive, piratical society, we have been governed by too simple and abstract notions of personality. Behind every social wrong are wrong people, but the wrongness of people is not the result of a simple will to evil. It is the result of undisciplined impulses, of undirected and misdirected energies, of violent inner conflicts or social collisions resulting in frustration and in repressed desires whose significance the individual does not often perceive, which make him as much of a mystery to himself as he is an irritation to others, concerning which he feels himself utterly helpless and against which all hortatory preaching and teaching are directed in vain.

In a chapter on "For Whom Christ Died in Vain"[7] Professor Waterhouse, of the University of London, attempts to answer the riddle of Judas. The poignancy and perplexity of that riddle every one of us must have felt. Here was a man who for many months was privileged to listen to the noblest teachings ever uttered, to hear the most faithful prayers which ever fell upon the ears and hearts of men, to live in close company with One who was so Godlike that ever since men have called him Son of God, and yet from all those regenerative influences Judas turned away to do the most dastardly deed in history, to betray the truest friend any man ever had, to plot against Christ as if he were a criminal, to hasten to a cross one who should have sat upon a throne. How could any man turn against Jesus in that fashion? What perversion of will could prompt a betrayer's kiss? One would have thought that Judas would have dropped dead in his tracks that night in the garden when, in the presence of the mob whose flickering torches sent the long shadows dancing under the olive trees, he took a kiss, the sacrament of love, and turned it into a seal of perfidy. Doctor Waterhouse thinks that behind that terrible event was a conflict in the soul of Judas between the aspirations awakened by Jesus and the avarice and pride that had been developed in his own heart by the experience of life. Instead of settling the conflict by confession and repentance, he began unconsciously to project his own sense of reproach upon Jesus. Instead of despising that in his own heart which stood between him and Jesus he transferred his contempt to Jesus until "There seems to be no reasonable ground for doubt that Judas projected his own wretchedness upon his Lord in one fierce act of uncontrollable hate."

That may not appeal to you as a satisfactory analysis of the deed of Judas. Anybody who has tried to analyze personality knows how difficult it is even when the person is before you and you have been told as much as he can tell you about himself. How much more difficult when he is only a dim figure in a very incomplete history! At any rate, it is an assured fact that the process thus described accounts for many of the present maladjustments between individuals and groups. In a multitude of lives are tragic conflicts. One part of the self condemns the thoughts, feelings, and actions associated with another part. Men desire to respect themselves. At the same time they are unwilling to face the dark reality of their partial self and to achieve self-respect by the conquest of that dark reality. So the sense of condemnation is deflected toward another. They denounce in someone else what they should denounce in themselves and by that denunciation achieve a feeling of virtue which enables them to live with themselves and others. Many of the belligerencies and betrayals of life are the result of personal faults which men and women have not learned to deal with directly and drastically. Some capitalists project upon laborers their own desire for ease, for wealth without arduous labor, for power, and denounce them as lazy, shiftless, grasping, and always to be resisted. Some laborers project upon capitalists their own aversion for their unpleasant tasks, their own "soldiering" on the job, and see them only as parasites and pirates. An eminent sociologist affirms that people "become radical because in their own personal life they have suffered or are suffering from conditions which they do not wish to face squarely. Instead of recognizing their own emotional disturbance and their own loss of contentment they turn their restlessness and dissatisfaction outward and create in society a theory of straw against which they can express their hostility. . . . They are most happy when finding fault, since by the process they relieve themselves from their own inner disturbance and . . . from their own sense of inferiority."[8] Much of the suspicion, hypercriticism, antagonism, which spoil our fellowships and make co-operative efforts difficult, and even impossible, are not the outcome of sheer perversity but are an escape from inner conflicts by the unconscious projection upon others of our own failures.

We meet people who are cruel toward their associates in business, toward outsiders, even toward their friends. They could never be persuaded of their cruelty nor turned from it by sermons or private admonitions. It is unconscious and has its roots in some fundamental frustration. "The farmer who would rather be a banker, the artisan who craves mental rather than manual labor, the housewife who is a frustrated artist or musician,"[9] are very apt to be cruel. They are not finding an outlet for their native skill but are performing daily drudgery. They are therefore at war with life itself and their cruelty is simply the inevitable expression of that permanently warring mood.

We are familiar with the domestic or ecclesiastical or educational or social tyrant who insists on making people over after a pattern which pleases him, who likes to dictate policies and programs and romances and careers. Such tyranny will never vanish as the result of either precept or example. It is the outgrowth of a disappointed ambition which is seeking in others a fulfillment denied itself. Here is a picture given by another psychologist. A father insists on his boy's taking a classical education with plenty of philosophical studies, wanting him never to be hurried but always to have plenty of time for quiet thought. But the boy proves to be a rollicking extrovert whose only interest is in popular, scientific experiment. Clashes of the will begin early. When the time comes for college, hostilities become open. The boy chooses a technical school, the father a small college where the classics are venerated. The father wins, for he pays the bills. The boy goes away in a state of rebellion, sows and reaps a terrible crop of wild oats, gains a most unsavory reputation, finally graduates and goes out into the world with an attitude of rebellion toward authority and ideas of self-aggrandizement which make him a social problem.[10] The story is told not for the sake of the boy but for the sake of the father. That father is not a fool nor a knave but one who has been sacrificed to economic pressure, has been denied the quiet hours which to him are real living. So, frustrate in the personal realization of life's real meaning, unconsciously he seeks realization through his son. His tyranny with its dreadful result is the outcome of his own ungratified ambition masquerading under the name of love and unselfishness, seeking an outlet in the boy which he did not have in his own career.

These illustrations taken almost at random from a broad category of conflicts within the self and between the self and its environment, resulting in great personal and social injury, are the beginning of a revelation of the complexity of the situation confronting anyone who attempts to make or remake personality. They represent a wide range of personal ailments which must be cured before a human society can be evolved which in truth can be called the kingdom of God. They portray ailments which can be cured or, better, prevented, but not by the naïve assumptions and more naïve strategies which have been employed in the pulpits and churches of the land. One hundred and fifty years ago Mr. Wesley preached a sermon on "The Causes of the Inefficacy of Christianity." "What a mystery is this," he says, "that Christianity should have done so little good in the world!" His reasons are interesting: first, because it is so little known not merely in heathendom but in Christendom; second, because it is so little practiced. He estimated that not five hundred among the fifty thousand Methodists then existing kept some of its most fundamental rules. That was about one per cent. Mr. Mencken probably would say that that is too high a percentage even for our day. But these replies leave the question still unanswered. The efficacy of Christianity should be in its ability to inspire practice. Why has it not done so? You probably have your reasons. Certainly, this is one: Christianity has not done more for men and women because we have not known Jesus or the human heart well enough to bring the transforming, captivating values that are in him to bear upon the native impulses which are the raw stuff of personality, in such a way as to direct those impulses into activities which shall be internally harmonious and socially useful and in unity with the good will of God. The great need of the hour is for a more comprehensive approach to personality, a more nearly adequate and sympathetic understanding of its problems and needs and possibilities than at present characterize the agencies of the church and especially the ministry.

V

Only thus can personality find its fulfillment and only thus can Christianity justify itself. "The real test by which both Jesus and Christianity are to be judged is the psychological test; ability to call out the devotion, mobilize the energies, unify and enrich the personalities of all men everywhere."[11] If Christianity maims personality, turning men and women into pallid ascetics who are afraid of life and incompetent to meet the demands of a complete human life; if it warps personality, sending out into the world dry-as-dust intellectuals or lachrymose emotionalists or spineless sentimentalists whose one passion is to feel good whether they are good or good for nothing; if it stifles personality, bequeathing to psychiatry a host of suppressed individuals who are restless, dissatisfied, frustrate, neurotic; if it fails to evoke man's highest potentialities, to bring him to the most complete self-realization possible in his environment; if it does not make him fit for high endeavor and for a place in a progressive society, it is not serving the needs of life and cannot be the final religion.

When I began the ministry, someone placed in my hands a book, the contents of which have gone from memory with a single exception—the profound conviction of the author that the next great debate in Christianity would be, not over the question of creation (the debate between Darwin and Moses was settled), nor about inspiration (historical criticism had won the right to be heard even about the sacred scripture), but about Jesus. That conviction has proved to be a prophecy. For a number of years now there has been a serious, searching inquiry into the place which Jesus ought to have in our teaching and preaching and thinking and living. Some of the discussion has been concerned with the metaphysics of his person—was he human or divine, man or God? Some of it has had to do with his ethic—will it work in an industrial society or in any human society? If the effect of that ethic on human personality was considered, it was only indirectly—what kind of a personality would be the result of a social order builded upon the teachings of Jesus? The conviction of many has been that we can have full-fledged persons only in a perfect society. The truth of that conviction we have already recognized. But it is time that we began to think more seriously and intelligently about the relationship of Jesus to the making of persons. For we must be about that business *now*. We cannot wait for a perfect social order to begin to create persons. Human beings are all about us. Many of them will be dead ere many changes occur, even in this era of experiment and adventure. If they are to become persons, they must have our assistance *now*. As preachers of Jesus, have we anything to offer them? I do not mean, have we anything that will make life a bit easier? I am not greatly concerned about that. In that respect Thomas Carlyle spoke the last word: "Foolish soul, what act of Legislature was there that thou shouldst be happy? . . . There is in man a higher than Love of happiness; he can do without happiness and instead thereof find blessedness." Our task is not to provide joy rides for the bored, nor to make life simple for the perplexed, but to create persons who by their mastery of the complex and the commonplace can here and now enter into the company of the blessed. Henry Drummond was a name to conjure with among students of a previous generation. Professor Peabody says that acquaintance with him was the most exhilarating incident of his academic life. Beginning with a passion for Ruskin and Emerson and a great interest in geology, he encountered Dwight L. Moody, received a new birth and a new mission, became not a teacher of science but a messenger of Christ to the liberally educated young men of his day. Professor Peabody writes: "If a saint must be a stern, grim, ascetic figure, with a visible halo and a dehumanized manner of life, then Henry Drummond cannot be counted among the beatified; but if there is room among the holy for joy in life, for courage in adventure, for delight in God and for the beauty of holiness, then this gallant, gracious, guileless gentleman whom his companions called Prince, should long be remembered among the saints of the world." Toward the making of persons like that, princely persons, true sons of God, the only kind of saints worth adoring, must we contribute if we are to justify our existence.

CHAPTER III

THE SECRET OF PERSONALITY

"AND the Pharisee stood and prayed thus with himself: Lord, I thank thee that I am not as other men are." But he was. The only difference between him and many other men was that he did not know that there was no difference. He was like other men in the one respect in which he was sure that he was unlike them—his ignorance of his true self. If it had not been such a tragedy, it would have been convulsive comedy—that man standing there, his face uplifted toward the heavens, his countenance aglow with self-satisfaction, his voice vibrant with pride, his gesture of prayer belied by the evident conviction that he did not really need to pray. Such self-ignorance could easily become the occasion of satire if one were in search of a subject and cared not for humanity. But to one who loved men as Jesus did and who knew the havoc self-ignorance can work, the sight of a man, boasting an attainment which was not really his, blind to motives which were wrecking his life, must have been the occasion of deep and devastating grief.

The Pharisee was not a rare phenomenon in

his generation. He is not unique even in ours. We may not be cursed with his pride; I wonder if anybody is proud these days. But we are afflicted with his blindness. Schopenhauer, taking his accustomed promenade at Frankfort-on-the-Main, was approached by a total stranger who had been attracted by the philosopher's unusual appearance and manner. Without any introduction, the curious visitor blurted out the eager question, "Who in the name of fate are you, anyhow?" Lifting dreamy eyes until they met those of the questioner, Schopenhauer replied somewhat sadly, "Alas, I only wish I knew myself." It was not philosophic caution merely which spoke thus; it was the sagacity of one who was wise enough to know that he did not know. If we were not so impressed with appearances, not so ready to assume that because we are ourselves we know ourselves, we too should answer quickly though confusedly to anyone who asks us "Who are you?" "Alas, I only wish I knew myself." The plausible explanation we give for our actions is often as remote from the real cause as a congressman's defense of his vote is from the true reason for it. In neither case may there be conscious hypocrisy—though sometimes one needs considerable charity to include some congressmen in that statement. But, certainly, in many of our actions, whether we be politicians or just human beings, there is ignorance of the actual motives at work. One honest soul was confronted not long ago with the question, "Why did you do that?" and, after a moment of serious quandary, replied frankly and rather mournfully, "I don't know why I did it." It is a confession which would be heard more often if we were less eager to justify ourselves and more willing to face the perplexing reality of our own personalities.

Nor are we much wiser in regard to others. We are very quick to judge the motives which inspire the deeds of our fellows and often we administer a rough-handed sort of justice in our appraisals. If we see a bandit robbing a bank, we may assume that he wants money. And if we are aware of the presence of an army of lobbyists in Washington, we are at least partly justified in the conclusion that they are there not for the public good but for private gain. But behind the loaded gun of the bandit there is more than a desire for money; there is a long train of experiences, some of them forgotten by the bandit himself, which have warped his personality until the will to live has become a will to rob or even kill. And behind the little black satchel of the lobbyist are experiences too which have taken the elemental drives of human nature and made of them not an artist or a philosopher but a social leech who knows where the blood is and is determined to get it, whatever happens to the body of the nation. Before either bandit or lobbyist can be changed into some more useful type of citizen, and before others now in the cradles and colleges of the nation can be saved from the pursuit of similar careers, we shall need to know more about the nature of personality, its perils and possibilities, than we do now.

I

(1) Some of our contemporaries regard man as very largely the creature of instincts, his main problem, as also the one hope of his fulfillment, being an outlet for those instincts on one plane or another. O'Neill characterizes Christianity as a calamity because it surrounds the instincts with limitations and denials. He would exile Jesus and enthrone Pan, the god of uninhibited human nature. There are many "Impuritans" who have broken into print, who have made civilization the butt of a joke, who conduct slumming parties under the delusion that they are giving young men a trip into Paradise, who do not know the difference between the whiteness of leprosy and the whiteness of purity, and who turn away from the Lamb of Calvary to establish what Wickham devastatingly calls "the cult of the goat." For the purpose of serious thinking, we can ignore these and all other advocates of expressionism, crude or

refined. The anarchy and disillusionment which attend all such coronation of impulse are quite sufficient to answer any claim urged in their behalf. The real threat to any comprehensive and workable view of personality comes from those who recognize that our natural impulses can not be permitted to run amuck, that life can not be intrusted either to a democracy or an aristocracy of instincts, that there must be some discipline resulting in some harmony and some refinement of expression. But they fail to realize that man is more than a bundle of primitive energies seeking an outlet. They do not reckon with reason and its demand for consistency, with the æsthetic self and its demand for beauty, with the sense of moral obligation and its stern judgments, with man's intimations of the Infinite and his capacity for religion. They biologize man and liquidate manhood in the process. They try to construct persons out of primitive urges and inevitably fail in the undertaking. They fail because, if it were possible by some process not personal to link the sex impulse to creative labor, the power impulse to some form of social service, the craving for comradeship to some movement for intercreedal or interracial or international good will, we might have socialized robots but we would not have persons. By associating the offer of meat with the sound of a bell, John Watson found that by and by a dog's mouth would water at the ringing of the bell even though the meat were not present. And he, and some others, leaped to the conclusion that making a man's mouth water, metaphorically speaking, at the sound of a church bell, or setting a soul panting after virtue, were simply adaptations of the same process, and that the difference between a dog, say, and E. Stanley Jones is that the missionary to India has a greater capacity for reconditioning than the dog. But a reconditioned animal is not a human being. There is something more in the picture at the beginning and at the end of the process of making personality than there is in the training of the most acute of the subhuman species.

(2) The assumption of too many preachers, teachers and parents, has been that correct ideas are the only need of the self, that right action will follow knowledge and that the consuming purpose of all lovers of humanity should be to exile false ideas from the minds of men and in their place instill true ones. Argument, advice, instruction, have been exalted as the saviours of life. Pulpits have become scholars' desks; sermons, pageantries of ideas; preachers, walking encyclopedias, though often much abridged editions; pastoral visits, the visitation of a systematic theology; public prayers, the exposition of the preacher's

notions about God or the report of a Committee of One on the State of the Church.

He would make war on history who repudiated the power of ideas. In a real sense history has been the march of ideas, sometimes slow and painful, sometimes compelled to retreat before the fierce onslaught of human passions, sometimes halted by the legions of economic necessity, sometimes apparently buried in the dust of defeat by institutions which have hated ideas as if they were the very devil, sometimes compelled to go into winter quarters by blinding blizzards of ignorance—but always surviving defeat and apparent death and at the first opportunity resuming the march across the field of human life. One cannot read a book like Alfred North Whitehead's *Adventures of Ideas* without being impressed by the surviving and transforming power of a great idea. Man is not merely a hungry animal perpetually on the hunt for bread, nor a social animal forever seeking his mate, nor a fighting animal always in quest of combat. He is a rational being with an appetite for ideas and a capacity for responding to their call, wedding his life to them, fighting for their existence, even dying for them.

And certainly we do not want any restriction on the production of ideas or their distribution. We can sympathize unreservedly with the impatient auditor whose preacher, finding the chariot wheels of his sermonic eloquence dragging heavily and endeavoring to expedite his progress, lifted his hand heavenward with the dramatic supplication, "More power, Lord." The power was slow in arriving and the restless hearer exclaimed, "What you want is not more power but more ideas." What is needed in every region of American life from Hollywood to Washington, not forgetting newspaper offices and denominational headquarters, is more and better ideas. After a few visits to the movies, after a few interviews with industrialists who are frantically trying to steady the ark of democracy, after reading the comments of some editorial writers on the function of the ministry, after waiting in vain for a sign of some disposition to lead on the part of our official leaders in these days of the church's great opportunity, the advent of an idea is the occasion of a doxology. Too often must the pulpit itself confess that the people have come asking for bread only to receive a stone, and that not always gracefully given.

But, certainly, man is more than a brain in response to ideas. Certainly, ideas about things merely, about relationships, about ways of living, even about people, cannot in themselves unify a divided personality, restore a maimed one, fulfill a partial one. Ultimately, of course, every remedy for the ailments of personality, every nurture for the needs of personality, every incentive to personality-fulfilling action must approach one either as an idea or as an emotion associated with an idea or as a volition expressing an idea. We are so completely idea-beings that nothing can be done for us or with us without the aid or accompaniment of ideas.

There is no greater fallacy in dealing with people than the assumption that the logical presentation of ideas, especially about personal conduct and social institutions, will make of people persons. Too much of our preaching and teaching and church organization assume that. Once in a period of very great stress, when a personal conflict had destroyed my peace and was threatening my effectiveness, I turned to some books of sermons for help. I did not know where else to turn. So few things are being written to help people who want to become persons. The best fiction sometimes helps, if written by one who understands life and has power to dramatize what goes on in the human heart. History and natural science and sociological studies and essays are concerned with other matters. Preachers are supposed to be experts in human need and sermons are their great opportunity for ministry to that need. So to sermons I went in my distress. They were evidently the utterances of strong minds. One saw on every page evidences of culture, scholarship, social passion, faith in God. Their congregations needed never hang their heads in embarrassment over the mental sloth, the moral insincerity, or the earthiness of the man who stood in their pulpit. But, if those sermons were any sample, the people who sat in the pews must have come and gone Sunday after Sunday without finding that which would unravel the tangles in their personality or unchain their fettered powers or help them more truly to become persons. At least that was my plight after my eager quest. The discourses were full of arguments for world peace, full of indictments for social wrong, full of poetic appreciation of the virtues, full of eulogies of Jesus, full of affirmation that this is a spiritual universe, but the preachers did not seem to realize that men and women need something more than objective ideas in order to obtain integrated and balanced personalities. There is a place for ideas in the making of personality, an important place, but one must reckon with their concomitant emotions in the minds of one's hearers—emotions which may have no logical connection with the ideas and which thwart or even pervert the normal functioning of the idea. Before an idea can exert its redemptive power there must often take place a reassociation of ideas and emotions, a process of which we as preachers have been too long neglectful.

(3) Sometimes man is treated as an æsthetic being with a hunger for beauty and with a capacity for being redeemed by beauty from whatever ails him and released by beauty for whatever amplification and growth his native self can attain. Art and architecture and music and ceremony and liturgy are the schoolmasters to bring him, if not to Christ, at least to himself. That there is in man a love of beauty none would be so foolish as to deny save those cynics who reduce thought, love, aspiration, and everything to a biochemical reaction to environment. But the rest of us know that beauty is a unique spiritual experience in which as Archbishop Temple says, "In a single impression we receive what absolutely satisfies us and in that perfect satisfaction we ourselves are lost. Duration vanishes; the moment eternal has come."[1] We know too that both in the creation of beauty and its enjoyment there is a heightening and intensification of personality which, after the immediate experience is past, leaves us more truly persons. An English canon was showing me about the glorious Cathedral at Winchester one day. He told me the story of the sculptors who, paid but a pittance a day, wrought in imperishable stone until it achieved the delicacy and grace and aliveness of a garden flower. One looks back upon those unknown workers in stone and wonders about them, how they lived, how they died.

But about one thing he does not wonder; he knows that however poorly paid, however meager their dwelling and manner of life, they were more truly persons because they first felt, then wrought the beauty which conspired to create that shrine for centuries of worshipers. And one knows too that something happens to those who pause in wonder before that sacrament of beauty which makes them more capable of fulfillment because they have felt the loveliness which once stirred in bosoms and guided hands now gone to dust.

But man is not merely an æsthetic being who can find completeness through the ministry of beauty. There are needs in his nature which beauty cannot supply. There is a strife within which beauty cannot arbitrate. There are paralyses which beauty cannot heal. There are buried powers which beauty cannot resurrect.

(4) No attempt to understand personality can ignore the view now being vigorously championed by Karl Barth and his associates. He stoutly affirms that human nature as we see it has not within itself even "the makings" of the kind of personality we should seek for ourselves and others. He would accept literally Paul's diagnosis of himself, "I know that in me (that is, in my flesh) dwelleth no good thing." Man is viewed as a fallen creature. He has lost the image of God bequeathed to him at creation. Nothing is

to be gained by the study of psychology. "Psychologism" is one of the arch enemies of religion. It will reveal what man is but not what he ought to be. Looking within one will be more apt to find the devil than anything else. The only hope of ever becoming true persons, that is, real sons of God, is to have our human nature broken and humbled and then utterly changed, born again by a new creative act of God. Without that creative act all processes of culture will be merely the dressing up of animated dust. Positing an essential, qualitative difference between time and eternity, viewing man in his natural state as a mere partaker of time, we must depend on the eternal God to break through the wall which separates man from him, and by a miracle of grace lift man over into the realm where God lives. Personality is not man's self-fulfillment but God's divine bestowment.

That Barth and his followers are reaching after something which has its roots in the New Testament and that his utterances are a challenge to easy-going humanism, it would be difficult to question. Too frequently we have assumed that personality is a flower carrying within itself the secret of its own life and growth, forgetting that without sun and shower there can be only death and decay. But, on the other hand, I am not ready to admit that the flower has no contribution to make toward its own development or that a study of the flower will not help me to assure and hasten and enrich the bloom. Mere psychology will not produce persons; neither will mere theology, whether it be the new theology of crisis or the theology we have always known. What is needed is neither self-dependence nor self-despair; neither the ignoring of God nor the ignoring of self; neither the pathetic strainings of self culture nor the pious waiting for some "existential moment," but, rather, such knowledge of our needs and of God as will bring our needs to God and bring God into the midst of our needs, such understanding of personality and of Jesus as will help us to open even the most remote recesses of personality to the redemptive influence of the supreme person, in order that we may reach the stature of full manhood.

II

What a consummation that would be! It is our immaturity, our incompleteness, our crippled or undeveloped faculties, our half-and-halfness, our consciousness of being so much less than we might be, that breaks our hearts. So many budding talents fail to blossom. Sapling virtues never become trees. Glorious dawns of aspiration seldom break into days of action. Thrilling chords awakened by the fingers of circumstance die away and we are not able to recapture them or weave them into a symphony of life. Foundations laid deep and broad in the strata of our purposes await in vain the building that will take the promise of beauty and lift it cathedral-like to the skies. There is a sense, of course, in which our incompleteness is our pride. It is evidence of the illimitable possibilities of our human nature. It points toward the necessity of an immortality for fulfillment. Real man is never full grown in the sense that his task henceforth is merely one of maintenance and prophylaxis against decay. His finiteness stretches always toward infinity without reaching it. His humanity at its best moves toward God without ultimately achieving divinity. A squash is matured in four months, a sequoia in four thousand years, a solar system in four thousand million years, a soul never. How much greater the soul than squash, or sequoia, or sun!

But there is a difference between a personality which is incomplete because the period of full growth is only partly gone and one which has not reached the degree of completeness commensurate with its age. No one blames a baby for not being a sage or a saint, but there is reason for alarm when one who ought to be able to eat the meat and engage in the ardors of maturity still clings to the bottle and finds amusement in the rattle of infancy. Still more is there occasion for grief when he lives in a world of phantasy rather than reality, is governed by prejudice or passion rather than principle, is ruled by fears instead of faith, is under the spell of notions instead of ideals. And what shall we say of sick personalities who cannot play a man's part in the world, who do not even know what that part is? The aim of Christianity was and is to make men—poised, powerful, commanding, co-operative. That aim has been frustrated not because God has not tried, not because the riches of his glory in Christ Jesus have not been available, but because we have not understood personality in ourselves and others well enough to give God the assistance which he must have. Our fathers used to have two strange words which were frightful to repeat but which in contrast pointed to a great truth—monergism and synergism. Monergism meant that the task of making men of us was God's work alone; synergism, that without our co-operation God is as helpless as we are without him. Life very urgently points in the direction of synergism. God is willing but his willingness waits on man's wisdom, on man's mastery of the secret of personality.

That secret is still very much a secret as far as multitudes are concerned, as much as electricity was before the days of Franklin and Edison, or as the radio was before the labors of Marconi, or as antiseptics were before the discoveries of Lister. Even those who have been at pains to explore personality do not assume that they have unraveled the secret. "The paradox of personality is that it is the reality about which we know most and least. . . . We know most about it because it is really the only thing we do know, for all our knowledge even of the objective world is the content of our own minds and the interpretation we put upon it; we know least about it for it is the one reality which must be defined in terms of itself."[2]

Once everybody seemed to believe that psychology was about to deliver personality into our hands. Not much was expected from behaviorism. In its passion for objectivity and certitude it lost that about which we most desired certainty —thought, aspiration, conscience, love. And when it came to dealing with people it had to resort to the old formulas. I once asked one of the leading objective psychologists in America what he would do in attempting to influence people to action. He smiled and said, "A long time ago I heard an address on effective public speaking. The lecturer gave four rules: arrest the attention, convince the intelligence, stir the emotions, arouse the will. I can give you nothing better than that." About many other aspects of personality, behaviorism could offer us "nothing better" than the old prescriptions. But some of us did turn hopefully to analytical psychology. It used picturesque language and it had some clinical success. Freud and Jung and Adler divided the self into two compartments, the conscious and the subconscious, the drawing room and the cellar. The drawing room was the abode of the things we called our ideals, the reasons we assigned for our conduct, our acknowledged deities. The cellar was the hiding place of our reals, the actual causes of our conduct, the animal desires whose presence we refused to acknowledge but whose power actually controlled the household. Those who desired to understand personality in themselves and others were urged not to waste much time in the drawing room but to descend into the cellar. If they found the door locked, psychoanalysis had the key. The ladder of dreams, unlike Jacob's which mounted heavenward and on which the angels of God ascended and descended, the rather, led downward, and on it could be seen the imps of biological impulse which cavorted in the subconscious and from there made fools of us all. Preachers turned to psychiatry. The gospel of Freud threatened to displace the gospel of Jesus, psychoanalysis supplanted repentance, transference performed the work of regeneration—at least in the minds of some very earnest people. Great expectations were entertained of the new science.

But a new note of skepticism is beginning to be heard. Professor Babbitt wrote a little while before his death: "The psychoanalytical divine is about the worst *melange des genres* in the present age of confusion."[3] Professor Jastrow admits that psychology may not be a science. A recent writer in the *Atlantic Monthly,* Grace Adams, herself holding a Doctorate of Philosophy in psychology, avers of her own specialty: "It has renamed our emotions complexes and our habits conditioned reflexes, but has neither changed our habits nor rid us of our emotions. We are the same blundering folk that we were twelve years ago and less sure of ourselves."[4] Such skepticism as these statements reveal and as exists in the minds of those even less competent to pass judgment, has been almost inevitable. There is so much confusion in the field, such contradiction among experts. One has only to attempt to discover some generally accepted class of instincts or some intelligible definition of emotion to know why there should be such incredulity. One preacher whom I know too well threw down a book on psychology the other day after months spent in an effort to arrive at a clear conception of the nature and function of emotion and, as the book landed on the table with unmistakable emphasis, the weary student declared no less emphatically, "I do not believe anybody knows anything about it." Not only is the same term used in different senses by different writers but the same writer will frequently indulge in such inconsistencies of language that one begins to wonder if behind all this confusion of language there may not be a confusion of thought which is incapable of offering us any sure guidance into the mysterious depths of personality. There are some books written by psychoanalysists so full of sheer mythology, so subtle about simple acts of daily life, so sweeping in their categories of the abnormal, that the reader begins to wonder whether the author is mad or he himself ought not to apply for admission to some mental hospital before his friends find it necessary to put him there.

Our disillusionment with any one school of psychology and our disappointment with the inability of psychology in general to confirm its claim to be a science ought not to blind us to some knowledge which has been gained and some insights which had been achieved. Concerning many aspects of personal life we still see through a glass darkly. Why men do what they do is still often a mystery, not to irritated observers only but to themselves. Why they are what they are is sometimes known only to God himself. But we are beginning to comprehend some facts about ourselves which offer real assistance to the effort to achieve and help others achieve fullness of life.

III

We begin with a self, the raw stuff of human nature received at birth. The development of that self, the evolution of its capacities, the fulfillment of its possibilities, is the goal of human life, or ought to be. That goal is what we mean by personality.

Nothing that is discovered in the future is likely to modify essentially the conclusion that this self of ours is from the very beginning a purposive striving. It is not an inert mass of bones and muscles and nerves and brain waiting to be molded into a pattern fixed by its environment. It is not a mere capacity for response needing some stimulus to set it in motion. It is a striving. It is alive, active, aggressive. Our schoolbook history with a dramatic flourish pictured to us an Alexander, having conquered the known world at twenty-eight and having died, sighing for more worlds to conquer. Every one of us is *born* literally sighing for more worlds to conquer. There is an imperious restlessness which characterizes human life from the beginning. The self strives. It strives purposefully. At the beginning those purposes are few but they are well defined—food, protection, a tender touch and gentle word from mother or nurse. If these are not quickly fulfilled there is rebellion and bedlam in the nursery.

Deceit may succeed for a while, the pacifier may be substituted for the bottle, the self-rocker for mother's arms, but ultimately the real needs assert themselves and the coo of content is followed by a cry of rage. As the months come and go, needs multiply and become more conscious, but nothing that happens changes the essential picture of self at the beginning as a purposive-striving. Professor James long ago described the self as a "fighter for ends." Professor Ogden reiterates again and again that the self is dynamic, never a passive recipient of impressions from without. Professor Coe declares that the self is not an aggregate of elements but an organic whole capable of transforming self within itself; . . . initiative is everywhere present.[5] Psychoanalysis begins within a dynamic self and in its term "libido" expresses its conviction that the individual self is essentially life, energy, striving.

About that simple fact of purposive striving is woven the whole story of the mutilation or fulfillment of personality. What the self strives for and what it fails to strive for and how the strife is conducted, determine the quality of person which it ultimately becomes, the range of its powers, its bondage or freedom, its sickness or health, its anarchy or its unity, its capacity for isolation or fellowship, for independence and co-operation, for citizenship in the kingdom of God. Striving is always the result of the pressure of some need or needs. We begin with a few imperious needs which we have in common with everybody else. The beggar's child and the princess in her palace are alike here. Socrates and Jesus did not differ from the humblest man among us. But soon other needs begin to appear. It is the glory of human nature that it seems to have an almost inexhaustible capacity for the acquisition of new and richer needs. We pride ourselves on our ability through science to supply our needs. We should be more jubilant that we are capable of developing needs which lift us above the heritage of the cradle and ultimately demand not merely time but eternity for fulfillment. Whether heredity has anything to do with their appearance in some individuals and not in others is still a matter of debate. Mr. Wiggam, in his *Fruits of the Family Tree,* tried to convince the public that it has. But a biologist like Langdon-Davies denounces what he calls "the crime of Wiggamy," the effort to blame our ancestors for faults which have their origin in ourselves, and he declares that nature has rather well standardized the business of making individuals so that, whatever our ancestors, we all begin life with the same general average of qualities. However that may be, the important thing for us who are seeking a working philosophy of personality is to recognize that however they may be acquired there are soon imposed upon our simple, primary needs a whole complex array of needs, conditioned more or less by the environment in which we live, family influence, school experiences, associations in work and play. We are so made that almost any experience which is pleasant may create in turn a need. There was a man who lived all his life in a great city amid towering walls and belching chimneys and cobblestone streets and all the clutter and clatter of a metropolis, where the sun shone through a haze of smoke, if it shone at all, and stars were reduced to a blur by the density of the atmosphere which hung above the city's night. At last he was permitted to visit the country and enjoy for a few days green meadows and meandering brooks and the silence of the verdant woods and the splendor of star-crowned nights and the glory of days flooded with golden sunshine and melodious with the carols of happy birds. Then he went back to the city but not to contentment, for that experience in the country had done something to him. He needed what the country gave him and what he never knew he needed before that unexpected and ravishing holiday. We are like that. Needs lead to experiences but experiences beget needs. And the bewildering variety of needs of which we are conscious in ourselves and others is the outcome of an equally bewildering variety of experiences to which life introduces us. One of Professor Coe's shrewd observations is that you cannot compress the soul of the workingman, or of anybody else, into a single formula.

In that fact lies the richness of civilization but also the peril and promise of the individual. For needs determine life. Thought is occupied with them, emotion clusters about them, effort is made in their behalf. From that thought, emotion, and effort results personality. Charles Stewart Parnell ruled, an uncrowned king of Ireland, for ten years. At one moment of his career his biographer could write, "He had defeated all his enemies in detail. Forster had been crushed, the Pope repulsed, Mr. Gladstone conquered, the Tories shaken, the Liberals scattered and subdued. No war, no party, no force which had come into conflict with him had escaped unscathed."[6] England feared him. Ireland worshiped him. But, alas, when men write of him now, they must say, "From behind the misty Wicklow hills appeared the man of destiny whom Ireland had been awaiting for a quarter of a century and whom she has regretted ever since." "When he passed into the shadows, there fell a curtain whose sordidness promised that oblivion would be active as well as passive toward his memory."[7] And ere the curtain fell we see his mother bending over his silent form pouring out her grief over a disgrace and failure upon which the world had no mercy. And there was Lincoln. He too was a lonely spirit, ambitious, eloquent, a fighter for freedom, a champion of the people; but the star which rose in obscurity, set in splendor, and has ever since been the pride of a nation and a world.

> If Nancy Hanks
> Came back as a ghost
> Seeking news
> Of what she loved most;
> She'd ask first
> "Where's my son,
> What happened to Abe—
> What's he done?
>
> . . . . .
>
> Did he grow tall,
> Did he have fun,
> Did he learn to read,
> Did he get to town,
> Do you know his name,
> Did he get on?"[8]

He did learn to read, not pages only but the book of destiny. He did get to town and to Washington. He did get on, on into the hearts of his countrymen and of all true men everywhere. That little mother, had she been told, must have wept at the manner of his death, but her tears would have soon been dried when men revealed to her the glory of his life. Parnell—Lincoln! And the difference wholly one of needs native and acquired and the strivings with which those needs were answered.

Everyone in the course of a lifetime acquires needs which are unreal, fictitious, unrelated to the goal of personality. These pseudo-needs are often very plausible, very convincing. They create an unrest which apparently has no cure unless they are gratified. They sometimes deceive the very elect. An ex-governor of New York appears to protest against a ten-thousand-dollar tax which federal and state governments would impose upon him and piteously pleads that after he has paid the rent for his fifteen-room penthouse apartment he will have *only* thirty thousand dollars a year to live upon. His plea leaves us cold. The most of us would be perfectly willing to try to squeeze through a year on a fraction of that sum. So would he have been a few years ago. But six years in the governor's mansion at Albany created certain wants which succeeded in passing as needs. Many of our so-called needs, of things, leisure, entertainment, attention, are in reality wants, artificially created, unnecessary to the completeness of personality or the fullness of life. An exposé of their superfluous character and emancipation from them, so that thought and energy can be concentrated upon real needs, are major requirements for him who would reach the stature of a perfect man.

There are other needs which are truly human, essential and not accidental. Their realization would undoubtedly enhance the personality, give it flavor, richness, zest, poise, sensitiveness, and consequent power. The need for a mate is a real need. But often the satisfaction of this truly human need comes into conflict with the demands of other needs of the self or the demands of society. Personality is often wrecked by that conflict, and careers are ruined and social reverberations are set in motion as devastating as that which followed the downfall of Parnell, which "blew little less than a hurricane through the statecraft of England."[9] The problem of personality demands for a solution such wisdom as can take this and other needs of the self which cannot have an immediate and complete answer and provide a substitute which will require a minimum deprivation of this single aspect of the self and clear the way for a maximum satisfaction of other needs more important for the individual himself and for those with whose destinies his own is inescapably linked.

There are still other needs, native and acquired, which *must have* adequate treatment if the self is to achieve the kind of personality which is worthy of a place in time and eternity. Of some of them we are painfully conscious:

> "O for a man to arise in me,
> That the man I am may cease to be."

Of some others and sometimes the most essential, we are unconscious, either because we are hypnotized by pseudo-needs or because we have not explored our own selves or because we have not had those experiences which beget needs whose birth, maturity, and satisfaction represent the largest opportunity of personal growth and achievement.

The self needs *security,* not freedom from peril but a sense of permanence in the presence of peril. It needs *power,* for the sake of the task life has set, of the esteem of others, of the conquest of difficulty. It needs *truth,* not merely as the instrument for the achievement of selfish ends but just because there is something within which can be content only when it has found truth, when the world within and without is proven rational, when the disharmonies of error and ignorance are resolved into the harmonies of truth, when chaos becomes unity. The self needs to be able *to respect itself*. There cannot be a worse paralysis than the loss of self-respect. As long as we live and retain the capacity for self-criticism there will be that in our lives which we shall wish were not there and which we shall be trying to remove. But the very effort at removal reveals that self-respect is still present. Lady Macbeth, walking the floor at midnight, crying piteously, "Out, out, damned spot," revealed that there was a bitter antithesis between her horrible deed and her real self. In her very remorse over what she had done was evidence that there was something in herself which she reverenced and was trying to save from utter pollution. But Kipling's rankers had lost even that:

> "We are done with hope and honor,
> We are lost to love and truth,
> We are dropping down the ladder rung by rung;
> And the measure of our torment
> Is the measure of our youth,
> God help us, for we knew the worst too young."[10]

Without self-respect all is lost. The self needs an *ideal,* a cause, something or someone to which the whole self can respond, in which the greatest possible unification of all the interests of the self can take place, and by which the self can escape itself and by losing itself find itself. Finally the self needs constantly to be *transcending itself.* The security, the power, the truth, the self-respect, the ideal, sufficient for to-day, are not sufficient for to-morrow. Life is advancing and we must advance with it. To-day's good may become to-morrow's evil; to-day's freedom, to-morrow's slavery; to-day's ideal, to-morrow's anachronism. In a Danish village church, every time the worshipers passed a certain spot on the wall they bowed. No one knew why. They did it because everybody else did, and because their fathers had done it before them. Then one day someone scraped the whitewash off the wall and found beneath a picture of the Madonna. Three hundred years before, that Madonna had been painted there. Then there was a reason for reverence. But for centuries, though the picture was covered with whitewash, the bowing went on just the same, as an inexplicable social habit. Personality is often bound by habits and customs, the reason for which no longer exists. Unless one achieves the art of self-transcendence he will live a hampered, irrational, wasteful life. The Greek ideal of being ourselves must be supplemented by the Christian ideal of receiving that which will make us more than ourselves at every stage of our pilgrimage. Who will help us in this fearful yet thrilling enterprise? Can Jesus?

CHAPTER IV

THE IDEAL PERSON

"THE world is a vale of soul-making." Sometimes souls are made. Too often they are marred. God must have infinite patience to have watched this process of making and marring all these centuries and still permit it to continue. It can be only because he has unlimited time and unguessed resources and unrevealed strategies by which to correct the failures of these three score years and ten. Olive Schreiner once said that she would hate to be God and be compelled to see in one sweep of vision all the pains and miseries and heartbreaks which around the world at any one moment afflict men and women and children. We turn away in horror from a single bloody accident, a lover standing in tears by the grave of his sweetheart, a mother huddling her hungry, shivering brood in emaciated, ragged arms, a trench filled with the bloated bodies of soldiers. But God cannot turn away. He must see not one tragedy but all the devastation wrought by disease and fire and war and poverty and death. What a strong heart he must have to behold it all and not die from sheer grief! But even more terrible must be the never-ending story of frustrated lives, of capacities perverted, of abilities stifled, of the promise of beauty and goodness perishing in a welter of ugliness and evil, of multitudes who, with a little wiser management, might have known freedom and gladness and power and creative splendor but who, lacking wisdom, are slaves and misanthropes, and paralytics and roustabouts. Pain is a circumstance in comparison with these mutilations of personality. We get over toothache. We survive heartbreaks. But we must live with ourselves now and forever. And God must live with us. The old doctrine of hell envisaged a situation which was harder on God than it was on man. For each man suffered the woe of his own wretchedness, while a God, conscious of all, if he had any heart, must suffer the woes of all. But wherever we may be before and after the pale rider on the white horse passes our way, we are within the compass of the life of God, and therefore God has either to endure or rejoice in us while we endure or rejoice in ourselves. We get excited about war and disease and poverty and death. We ought to get more excited about their terrible effects on personality, and still more about the frustration of personalities, which are the result, not of an invasion of either of the four horsemen of the apocalypse, but of our mishandling of ourselves.

We were saying in our last lecture that the self is essentially purposive striving; in the beginning a striving to satisfy a few elemental needs, later to answer needs both native and acquired. Some of those needs are artificial; some real and important but incapable of fulfillment in one's immediate situation; some of them indispensable to the realization of the abundant life. But always the self is striving, wisely or unwisely, to satisfy these needs. It has been our supreme failure as preachers and teachers and parents and captains of our own souls, that we have not recognized the purposively striving character of the self. We have attempted to deal with our own self and the self in others as if it were a more or less passive or plastic something, waiting to be molded by the fingers of decision into pleasant shapes—our chief problem being to decide what those shapes should be. And we have had as little success as the Sunday-school teacher who prepared her lesson as if she would have before her a crowd of boys who would be hushed into silence at the sound of her voice, impressed by her ideas and easily persuaded to give those ideas hands and feet; but who actually finds as many squirming bits of irrepressible human energy as there are boys, each one wanting to do everything else except what she wants done, their heads buzzing with ideas which they want to translate into action not merely when the lesson is over but then and there; more interested in swimming holes than in saints, in the crack of the baseball bat than in the crack of doom, utterly unable to understand why there should be on the calendar a day of rest when they are not conscious of being tired. Horace Mann used to tell about a boy who came to the close of a school day with pent-up energies which had reached the exploding point. Unable to restrain himself longer, he whistled outright. "John," said the teacher, "was it you who whistled?" "No, sir," replied John. "Henry," said the teacher, "didn't John whistle?" "Yes, sir," said Henry. "John," said the teacher, "how dare you say you did not whistle?" "I didn't whistle," said John, "it whistled itself."[1] John was not smart, he was right. When we deal with a self, our own or others, we are dealing with a something which whistles itself, which has initiative, which is aggressive, which is forever breaking into action because of inner pressures. Unless resolution and teaching and preaching and discipline and prayers and principles and programs and causes and ideals can be related to those inner pressures, they cannot make an appeal and they will not modify the self or materially affect the life or enter into the stuff of personality. The striving will go on, but it will be either a blind striving after genuine values or a shrewd striving after fictitious values, and in either case the results in personality will be disastrous. But, on the other hand, such is the nature of the self that it can be emancipated from the tyranny of pseudo-needs; it can be appeased with substitutes for those needs which though genuine are immediately beyond attainment; it can develop new secondary needs out of its primary ones. Thereby its strivings may become drivings in the direction of ideals, the motivation toward duty and goodness and truth. As these values are achieved, personality will find its fulfillment.

I

The question always before us, then, is this, What am I proposing to myself and others which is related to fundamental needs of human nature or which may become a vitalizing need whose achievement will mean the enrichment of personality and its progress toward perfection? It is a question which in the Christian Church has had its traditional and ready and sometimes complacent and too facile answer in Jesus. Preachers have pointed to Christ and have said, "Look unto him and be saved." They have preached Jesus in one fashion or another, have argued about him much and eulogized him with sonorous rhetoric and have repeated and interpreted or misinterpreted the story of his words and his life and his death. Laymen have listened and sometimes have been convinced, and either wistfully or hopefully have waited for something to happen to them in response to what they have called faith, which would transform and liberate them, endow them with moral power and spiritual insight and make them real persons in the kingdom of persons. It would be calumny to say that nothing has happened as the result of all this. Much has happened to redeem life from its sordidness, to open prison houses of shame and fear, to deliver the captives of evil habit. The person of Jesus is so splendid that even a partial glimpse of him leaves one a bit more a person than he was before. He is so like us that, if opaque preaching and cloudy theology let even a little of him be seen, he makes his own appeal. Our hearts recognize his kinship with us. We are interested in spite of preachers and theologians. He is so unlike us that, having fascinated us by the fellow feeling he awakens, he arouses aspiration by the very spectacle he presents of one so like us, nevertheless being so far beyond us. We begin by feeling at home with him. We soon pass into a consciousness that he is different. We end by wanting to be different ourselves, that we may feel at home with him again. That has always seemed to be the history of any individual or group of individuals where Jesus has had any chance at all.

But we must sorrowfully confess that there has been too little of such history. The recent literary wail, "God Save the Church," the fierce protest of Dick Sheppard in *The Impatience of a Parson,* are but passionate outbursts of what has been in many souls when they have studied the lives of churchmen and have asked themselves what all our sermons and sacraments are doing to make persons. It is impossible not to see, "the blindness to beauty, the indifference to truth, the idolatry of mere possessions, the frivolity of purpose," the lack of poise, the nervelessness, the spinelessness, the antitheses between creed and practice, the quasi-neurotic character of many who belong to the Christian Church, listen most regularly to its sermons, fight most bitterly for the faith once delivered to the saints. Is it because Jesus merely awakens desires we never can forget but is not adequate to all the demands of human nature? Is it because he makes us wish we could be like him but leaves us wallowing in a sunken nature and a sordid society which make such likeness forever impossible? Or is it because Jesus has not been understood?

II

There have been and are many voices which affirm that Jesus even when understood has little to contribute to the making of personality. Nietzsche affirmed "The whole of improving morality, including Christian morality, has been a mistake. . . . It has all been decadence under another name." And Professor Dewey, in language less vitriolic but not less positive in its denials when all the implications of his words are understood, said, "I do not think early Christianity has within it even the germs of a ready-made remedy for present ills and a ready-made solution of present problems."[2] In one of the best books ever written on the problems of personality, *The Normal Mind,* the author quotes approvingly a code of mental health advanced by another, one of the ten rules of which is "Shun the New-England conscience." It would, of course, be quite a leap of the imagination which would attempt to make the New-England conscience synonymous with Jesus but one thinks he detects in that rule considerable nervousness about the thing which the Puritans and Jesus had in common. There appeared several years ago a cartoon of the Judgment Day. Two companies were portrayed—Christians who were ticketed for heaven, the rest who were evidently going in an opposite direction. The Christians were a pale, pinched crowd of semipersons who looked as if life for them had been a cramping, devitalizing business. The other folks were a gay-looking group who were

process whereby, as the result of his receiving into his own heart all the penalty due all the sins of all humanity, each one of us may receive judicial release from penalty, a change of juristic status from that of men condemned to die to that of recipients of divine clemency, and thus we may become heirs of heaven instead of criminals on the way to hell. The significance of Jesus was as a sacrificial victim whose sufferings made such a process of redemption possible. The emphasis was upon his death rather than his life, upon the shame of his cross rather than the glory of his character, upon the awfulness of his punishment rather than the awe of his personality. Of course it was always affirmed that he was good, so good that he had no sins of his own for which atonement was needed. But the nature of that goodness, incarnate in the fullness of a perfect personality, and its significance to all who are striving to become persons, was almost lost from view. Men did not study Jesus or preach him with the purpose of discovering and disclosing his fulfillment of our human nature but as the key figure in a plan of salvation, a scheme whereby the weaknesses of human nature were atoned for and we were made partakers of the divine nature. Even such an interpretation of Jesus was not without its value. Those whose philosophy or lack of philosophy permitted them to accept it found a sense of security; the wrath of God no longer hung over them like a Damocles sword. There was a certain increment of self-respect; if Jesus died for them, there must have been something in them worth dying for. There were feelings of gratitude awakened which became the motivation of a better life. Many of them sang and meant what they sang, "I'll live for him, who died for me." There were some values acquired and conserved, but there were many needs of the person which remained untouched because the personality of Jesus which might have answered those needs was veiled behind a scheme of redemption. He was not our human example but the divine victim. He was lifted before us, not as an illustration of what we might become but solely as a revelation of what God is. His business was not to fulfill us but to break us and then to translate us into another category of being altogether. But even the values which once accrued as the result of such a conception of him have ceased to be possible for many. The thought world which gave it standing has passed away. God is no longer looked upon as Judge but as Jesus actually portrayed him, as a Father. Man's sin is not the violation of a code whose integrity must be preserved at all costs but, rather, his failure to be a true son of his Father. God is neither eager nor bound to punish; the idea of punishment is obsolescent even among men. We do not punish offenders; we try to discover what is wrong and set them right. Even if God were a Judge bent on punishment, the idea of transference of punishment is very difficult to connect with eternal justice. Jesus' death was not a judicial stroke; it came about very naturally as a result of the conflict between what Jesus was and the selfishness of his contemporaries. Jesus as a process cannot therefore lead us to the fulfillment of personality.

He has been presented as a producer of mystical joy and peace, not a peace which is the result of the harmonization of hitherto conflicting interests, not a joy which comes from the answer to felt needs, but a joy and a peace magically wrought within the soul of one who met certain formal requirements such as repentance and confession and faith. Popular songs assured multitudes that they might have "sunshine in the soul" and be "happy all the day," and popular preaching did not elucidate the process beyond an assurance that it would come somehow if they turned to Jesus. There is sunshine in the soul when that soul is reorganized about Jesus as a center. There is happiness when the torn, anarchic, thwarted self finds through him the secret of internal unity. But it is not a result magically attained and the effort to attain it without paying a price, both in self-knowledge and in the knowledge of Christ, has led men and women into a world of fantasy, where self-induced moods, achieved through the opiate of suggestion and under the spell of moral blindness, have made mockery of real Christian manhood and womanhood and have given us men and women who were incapable of exchanging prejudice for truth, of heroic answer to the call of duty, of sacrificial service to their fellows.

The presentation of Jesus has so often been a parody. Bernard DeVoto, writing of Strachey as a biographer, says, "His Chinese Gordon could never have worn a uniform; his Florence Nightingale is only a series of epigrams about a nurse. Literary people should not be permitted to write biography. The literary mind . . . is the mind least adapted to the utilization of fact."[3] One might say equally of many biographies and many descriptions of Jesus, "Their Jesus could never have borne a cross. They have given us only a series of epigrams about a Galilean teacher. They have produced literature; they have not let us see a life." His holiness has been described as a perpetual judicial threat. His teachings on humility have been twisted until they have become the enemy of self-respect; on self-sacrifice, until they have seemed a demand for self-mutilation; on the will of God, until the will of man has been relieved of all worth and responsibility. His truth has been offered as a final orthodoxy which has frightened men away from further quest and has thus denied them an experience without which personality must always be a dwarfed, pitiful affair. His work has been pictured as a finished work rather than, as in Luke's more lucid phrase, "What Jesus began to do and to teach"; and the result has been a quietism which has denied personality the challenge and stimulus of a cause. He has been so entangled in the customs and habits of thought of his contemporaries and in the theologies and the world views of his immediate followers that he has seemed utterly inadequate for a scientific, socially-minded generation and therefore incapable in himself of being that Ideal to which the modern man can commit himself and by which he can be unified and in which he can find himself.

IV

If we are to be persons and help others to become persons, we must recover the ideal person. Who was he? To what Jesus are we to turn? The Jesus of history? Surely. But who is he? It is not enough to refer the questioner to the New Testament and say, "There he is—four portraits of him drawn by master hands. Study them and you will know what manner of man he was." We must turn to the New Testament. We cannot turn elsewhere. Secular history took little account of him. We must find him in sacred lore or not at all. But every student knows that there are serious difficulties in reaching back through the sacred page to the sacred person, difficulties arising out of differences in the records themselves, out of the distance between the records and the events they describe, out of the credulities of the age in which the events occurred and the records were written, out of the character of the events themselves, events like the stilling of an angry sea, the feeding of the five thousand with a basket of food, the raising of the dead, events which seem to the scientific mind a collection of fairy tales. Above all is the mystery of the central figure himself. As there presented, he escapes our normal categories and makes men wonder whether our categories need revision or whether the figure ever really lived except in the phantasies of an overwrought religious imagination. Professor Scott affirming, "There are few lives of antiquity of which we know anything like so much," nevertheless admits "the real difficulty consists in the nature of the life itself; . . . there is no standard by which we can judge him. We know nothing of the motives and inward experiences which lay behind his visible action. This knowledge could not have been conveyed to us by any record, and it is our want of it which makes the life so mysterious."[4] As a result of the effort to penetrate the inconsistencies and obscurities of history and sift the wheat of reality from the chaff of fancy, great and honest minds have arrived at various and often mutually exclusive conclusions about Jesus. Weiss and Deissmann and Loofs and Bultman and Wrede and Schweitzer in Germany, and Baillie and Bundy and Bacon and Case and Denny and Easton and Scott in America, not to mention a host of scholars in France and England and elsewhere, have probed the past and emerged from their research with a confused and confusing result. After all this study the editor of the *Christian Century* complains that up to date our scholars seem to fall short of giving us a Figure who moves with verisimilitude in his immediate environment.

We, preachers, have been less than frank with our people about this crucial matter. Unwilling to give doubt standing room in our pulpits, we have created greater doubts by the assumption of a certainty which our intelligent hearers know we do not possess. Afraid to confess our limitations, as if our confession would be confusing, we have let loose a more troubling confusion by our abstract exhortations to "come to Jesus" when those who hear us have such vague notions about Jesus' position in the moral hemisphere that they do not know in which direction to start in order to arrive anywhere in his neighborhood. We have taken a Book, over which the world's brightest minds have pored and with whose problems they have wrestled, and we have placed it in the hands of earnest seekers after life without giving them a key to its treasures; the only possible explanation being a conviction that the untutored mind may safely rush in where the angels of scholarship fear to tread. We have forgotten that our people read other books besides the Bible and hear other voices than our own. We have tried to create faith by ignoring questions. We have thought to honor Jesus by leaving him in a fog in which spiritual ardors have been chilled and multitudes have lost their way.

We, ourselves, have come to the conclusion that some things written about him are not true, and we are glad that they are not. And yet we let our people continue to think that they are true and we wonder why they are not enthusiastic about him. We have found great help for the discipleship of his mind and heart in reading the records with a disciplined liberty which can say: "That does not sound like Jesus; he never said it. That does not look like Jesus; he never did it. Ah! that is like the man of Calvary and I take it to my heart." But we pass the Gospels on to our laymen with an all-or-nothing gesture which has refused them the right of discrimination or has not given them any clue to a method of discrimination. And the result has been often a reaction which said, "If it is all or nothing, then it must be nothing, for I cannot take it all."

The best men we know in Christendom to-day, men whose intelligence and character and social passion impel us to put on their heads the crown of leadership, are men who have painted their own portrait of Jesus out of the primary colors furnished them by the Gospels and who have made that Jesus Lord of their lives. They could not surrender to a vague mystical Jesus nor could they have been saved by a composite figure constructed out of the undifferentiated mass of Gospel narratives. They have used their historical judgment, their moral discrimination, their spiritual insight, to disentangle the real Jesus and have found in turn their judgment, discrimination, insight, quickened to new splendor. But we, discouraging anything like a critical approach to the history of Jesus, have wondered why men have not found him and become enthralled by him.

V

This preacher wants to take you into his confidence. He believes in Jesus, the Ideal which is the ideal for man's soul; which is capable of producing not merely the greatest happiness for which the psychologist pleads, but the most complete personality. He believes that in Jesus all the real needs of the self find at once that clarification and that satisfaction which will make of the self a real person. Whatever of personal fulfillment has come to this preacher has come as he has walked in the light streaming from that radiant Man of yesterday. Whatever personal frustration has visited him has been because in blindness or wilfulness he has refused to walk in that Light. But that Jesus who has meant so much to him and on whom he risks the future has not been the traditional Jesus of the unexamined records nor the poetic Jesus of religious fantasy. It has been a Jesus who rose up out of the records, who gradually bit by bit recreated himself out of authentic word and assured deed, who grew by a process of moral and spiritual assimilation, who was at first a central core of indubitable fact and then, like a magnet lifting iron filings out of a pile of sand, selected out of accumulated stories about him those which really belonged to him and took them up into himself. I do not know how else one can ever recover a figure of such antiquity. There was no science of history to scrutinize records. There were scarcely records, only scraps of writing, and here and there glowing memories. But there is more or less of unity in the characters of men, and the greater the man the more perfect the unity. So that if one can but learn a few basic determinative qualities about one so far away, those qualities become criteria by which one may judge all the narratives which survive oblivion. In a real sense the man rewrites his own history for us if we will only let him do so. It is because we have not been willing to let him do so, because we have been overawed by the canon of the New Testament and by doctrines of inspiration that we have had most of our troubles about the history of Jesus.

We do know some things about Jesus. We know that he lived, we know in part how he lived, we know why he died. The animating principles of his life and his death are ours beyond the shadow of a reasonable doubt. Knowing them, we are not at liberty to set him saying and doing things which we think a man of his type, living in a society like that of Galilee or Judæa, might have done. We must not create history. But knowing the kind of a Man he was, revealed in indubitable word and deed, we can at least cleanse his history of the accretions of tradition and misinterpretation. Knowing the kind of a Man he was, we can be rather sure that he did not destroy the herd of Gadarene swine nor rebuff the Syrophœnician woman who came to him for help, nor curse a fig tree because it offered no fruit to his hunger, nor send a disciple down to the lake to find a fish with enough money lodged in its throat to pay the temple tax, nor espouse the doctrines of the apocalyptics with their notions of a militaristic God. It is by this process of discovery of a central reality and the enthronement of that Reality in the seat of history that the person of Jesus has at last revealed itself before one preacher's mind. He knows the peril involved in such a process. He can appreciate the scorn with which a laborious student like Goguel speaks of the "host of literary men and philosophers" who are "advancing in good order to take possession of the territory abandoned by historians in their retreat."[5] Imagination and devotion cannot take the place of technique in the writing of history. But even Goguel confesses, "In order to understand the thought of Jesus we must have or must acquire the spirit of a Christian. Erudition is indispensable, but where there is nothing else an essential element is lacking. The Jesus whom it will paint will not be the real Jesus. . . . In order to understand Jesus the historian ought to have in himself something that is like Jesus."[6] There is something, therefore, to be said for the preacher who, filling his head with all the knowledge of historical research which it can absorb, nevertheless, at last, trusting to that in his heart which has kinship with Jesus, finally permits head and heart together to make a portrait of this elusive but also inescapable Man of Galilee. The most important question which can be asked of a preacher is, "What kind of a Jesus do you preach?" of a layman, "What kind of a Jesus do you follow?" We shall attempt in answer what Mr. Strachey has called a portrait in miniature.

The usual story of a life is summarized in deeds and words. Nor are we without benefit of such material in an effort to recapture the personality of Jesus. Miracle and chronology will long be in dispute but there is practical unanimity among students as to the picture of a Man who, after thirty years of comparative seclusion, was challenged by the ministry of John the Baptist and entered upon a career of teaching which aroused the antagonism of the religious orthodoxy of his day and finally brought him to a cross where he died on the spear point of hatred for his rebuke of religious formalism and fanatical patriotism; but who after his death, in some fashion full of mystery to us, convinced his disciples that he was not a dead prophet but a living comrade and inspired them to launch a campaign for the salvation of the world.

Concerning his teachings there is less unanimity, especially as to specific utterances. But there is little question that the central emphases are preserved to us; the true Fatherhood of God and the consequent brotherhood of all men; love as the only sufficient moral law; service the hall mark of greatness; forgiveness of others the condition of receiving the forgiveness of God; self-sacrifice, along with self-realization, the way to fullness of life; sincerity and reality the rule for all relationships between man and man and between man and God; the kingdom of God, that is, the reign of God *now* in the heart of the individual and ultimately in every human association—economic, political, international—the one worthy object of endeavor; eternal life as the heritage of all who prove themselves capable of entering into its meanings—a simple but comprehensive body of moral and religious teaching, consistent, revolutionary, inexhaustible in application but the practice of which may be begun now by men and women of every class and every clime.

Behind these words and deeds arises a personality whose very heartbeat we can feel. It is a psychically sound personality. Denials have been entered. Holtzman charges Jesus with being an ecstatic; Rasmussen, an epileptic; De Loosten, a paranoiac with characteristic delusions of grandeur; Bauman, a case of nerves. But such charges disappear like smoke before the west wind when facts and fair analysis appear on the scene. We are greatly indebted to Professor Bundy for his careful and comprehensive analysis both of the criticisms directed against the personality of Jesus and of the personality itself. His conclusions are convincing. Jesus was always the master, never the victim of his emotions; elation did not destroy reflection nor depression drive him to despondency and despair. "In his darkest hour he did not desert God but asked why God deserted him."[7] His intellectual life reveals powers of observation of the first rank linked with logical faculties of which any man might be proud. "The resourcefulness and play of Jesus' intellectual faculties in his encounters with his Jerusalem enemies still await their parallels in history."[8] There was no fixed idea, no single issue in his mind, but every evidence of an entirely normal consciousness. His will was characterized by perfect co-ordination. It was, "the will of the rational man, . . . the highest force which nature has developed, . . . the last consummate blossom of all her marvelous works."[9] Professor Bundy brings his admirable treatise to a close with this striking paragraph: "A pathography of Jesus is possible only on the basis of a lack of acquaintance with the course and conclusions of New Testament criticism and an amateur application of the principles of the science of psychiatry."[10]

The personality of Jesus was profoundly social. There was no aloofness, no hauteur, no cynicism in him. He loved people of all sorts—young children and old men, rich and poor, learned and ignorant. He loved people more than laws or institutions and was instantly at war with any rule or custom which hurt people or hindered their fullest life. But Jesus was also strikingly independent. He refused allegiance to sanctified tradition. He would not tremble even before a quotation from the Old Testament. His only final loyalty was to God and he believed that an enlightened conscience furnished a receptivity to the revelation of God's will which justified him in challenging even the weight of religious opinion of his day. He was decisive and dynamic in his choices. He was characterized by the most sublime trust in God the world has ever seen, and that trust gave him a repose and poise in the midst of a social turbulence which at times resembled nothing quite so much as a seething volcano. But trust in the care and grace and seeking love of God was balanced by a sense of personal responsibility which took tremendous risks in speech and action and packed into a few months of public labor more meaningful conduct than most of us put into a lifetime. Possessed of an unusually sensitive conscience yet he confronts us with the unparalleled spectacle of one who gives no evidence of having anything in his own life for which repentance was needed. The most critical acumen is compelled to say, "In none of [the words] which have come down to us can we find anything at all which can be construed as an expression of a sense of sin or penitence."[11] There was power there but power under control; there was joy there, not the facile, flimsy thing we call happiness, which is often rather irritating, but joy which was radiant; there was love there, such love as could inspire Paul's marvelous epic, the thirteenth chapter of First Corinthians. Jesus was human to the very fingertips; he knew what it was to be tired and puzzled and lonely and defeated. He was the kind of a man one could go to about anything. But there was something about him which was more than human. The most critical reading of the records cannot escape that sense of awe with which even his closest friends regarded him. It is written once concerning his friends that "they following after were afraid." It was the kind of a reaction men feel when they think of the holiness and greatness of God. It was a sense of the *numinous,* inexplicable but very real.

That is Jesus, not the Jesus of theological speculation, but the Jesus of history. Like you him or not? Is there any improvement you can suggest to a personality like that? Can anyone who seeks to grow a personality afford to neglect him? Granting the uniqueness of each self that comes to birth, and of the problems which confront such a self on its way to maturity; recognizing that there can be no blanket prescription for all souls any more than for all bodies, nevertheless if light is to come from anywhere on our quest for personality, it must come from one who in himself achieved such fullness of life as impels men to lay a crown of adoration upon a brow that was once crowned with thorns. We certainly shall not turn away from him to cynics or Bohemian rhapsodists; to men who can write smart things but cannot live great things; who can

> "Tear the Saints to pieces
> And label all the parts,
> And tabulate the secrets
> Of loyal, loving hearts;
> Whose reasoning is perfect,
> Whose proofs are plain as paint,
> Who have but one small weakness—
> They cannot make a saint."[12]

Rather, from all those, whose pertness nevertheless has not produced a personality anyone would ever covet, must wise seekers after maturity turn to him who in all centuries has made men want to be like him.

VI

The ministry of Jesus to personality has not been confined to the guidance which a historic splendor can bring to men and women of later centuries. There are two more convictions about him which have played a very important part in

Christian history, which need restatement for the life of to-day and which will appear again and again as we prosecute further our quest for personality.

One arises out of his peculiar relationship to God. His words have had so much weight with men because they have been accepted not as human conjectures but as the wisdom of God. His character has been comforting and inspiring because it has been regarded as a revelation of the character of God. "If Jesus, in his participation in human joys, in his fellowship with the faulty and the fallen, in his humorous criticism of the righteous, in his stern denunciation of the self-righteous, in his love of fine character, in his passion for truth and the welfare of men, in his power to cure the ills of mind and body, in his dependence on human friendship, in his majestic victory over defeat—if in all this, the historic Jesus is the true and living revealer of the transcendent God, how great is our hope!"[13] In the attempt to define the manner in which Jesus becomes the revelation of God, there has been much metaphysical speculation, much theological controversy, and sometimes a bitterness which has blasphemed the spirit of him whom we were attempting to describe. The human nature of Jesus has been submerged in a divine nature; or it has been described as existing side by side with the divine nature in one person. Jesus has been made synonymous with God, it being affirmed that the Ruler of the universe once became localized on this tiny fragment of star dust and lay as a Babe in a manger. He has been pictured as a true human struggling toward and finally achieving divinity. His oneness with God has been conceived now as an ontological, now as a moral unity. Such confusion was inevitable. If it were true that God once uncovered his mind and heart in a human life, the human mind would want to explain how it could happen and would seek explanation in categories congenial to its own experience and world-view. But it is significant that men of such different schools of thought, ranging from a trinitarianism, which is a thinly disguised tritheism, to a practical unitarianism, have nevertheless been compelled by the moral majesty and spiritual supremacy of Jesus to say that while we discover the footsteps of God in nature and in the minds of heroes and sages of the race, we come face to face with him in Jesus. Principal Garvie wrote: "What the relation of the historical manifestation in Christ may be to the eternal reality of God or to the present activity of God, I do not know, but I do know that any present experience I have of God is through and through mediated by Christ, his cross, and his spirit, and for me, therefore, the only knowledge of God which avails and satisfies is the vision of God in the face of Jesus Christ."[14] Professor Craig, far to the left of theological opinion, affirms, "Speculative solutions of the person of Jesus promised little to our generation so aware of the limitations of any transcendental knowledge. . . . If we follow Jesus because we find in him the most ultimate meaning we can discover, no further myths will add to his authority."[15] Such an ultimate meaning, such a conviction, that in Jesus, if anywhere, one finds God, while not inescapable any more than any ultimate truth is inescapable, nevertheless to some of us is the highest wisdom about history and human experience which we have encountered and is fraught with significance for those who are seeking the fulfillment of their personality.

The second arises out of his peculiar relationship to us. It has been given to a Jewish Rabbi, Solomon B. Freehof, to say it directly and succinctly: "He is still the living comrade of countless lives. No Moslem ever sings 'Mohammed, lover of my soul,' nor does any Jew say of Moses, the teacher, 'I need thee every hour.' The genius of Jesus is not one of doctrine nor of organization but is distinctly one of direct influence."[16] This is the Jesus whom we preach, a definite historical figure whose teachings and character rise out of the dim past in clear and convincing outline and who comes to us to-day to bring the good news of God and the sense of a living presence. To him we shall look in succeeding lectures for an answer to the quest for the secret of personality.

CHAPTER V

PERSONALITY AND SUCCESS

DR. JOSEPH COLLINS, shrewd observer of human life, once wrote this aphorism, "It is more important to live than to succeed."[1] With a nobler interpretation of that word "success," one may affirm with conviction, "It is more important to succeed than to live." From the standpoint of the psychology of personality there is but one real success—the matching of a mental image with reality. If one cannot match mental images with reality, he might as well stop living. He does stop living in any vital sense. He becomes "a ghost wandering on the winds of unfulfilled desire." If, on the other hand, one learns the art of matching mental images with reality, not only does life become full of zest and meaning, but, if the mental images are wisely chosen, he himself becomes a real person and a social asset.

I

That we are here confronted with a real need of the self a survey of human life makes very clear. The perversity of the child in doing the thing we do not want him to do is often the result of the fact that that very thing is at the time the only mental image which can be translated into action. Frustrate on every side by his own physical limitations or by adult discipline, he finds release and fulfillment in what to us is a hideous deed. One youngster, left in charge of a neighbor, was surrounded with a wall of "don'ts" which evoked a rebellion. The irate temporary guardian in sheer self-defense was compelled to incarcerate him in a dark closet. Immediately the little prisoner broke into such a torrent of cries that the neighbor, fearing a spasm for which she did not want to assume responsibility, unlocked the door. Whereat the ertswhile tearful young rebel marched out with a look of triumph and the proud declaration, "I was too much for you, wasn't I?" That conquest was the first idea which had succeeded in becoming history that afternoon, and the boy was thrilled and his soul was saved, psychologically, if not theologically. Unless images can become events in some normal fashion, events are likely to become disasters as far as youth is concerned. Domestic peace and the calm of the school are sometimes purchased at a terrible price.

The coming of adulthood does not essentially alter the situation. There is more power—physical, mental, economic—to do what one wants to do. But there are also more needs, a greater variety of mental images panting to become deeds. And there are new limitations arising out of one's position as a member of a complex society. Life, therefore, witnesses a constant evolution of strategies whereby the self may satisfy the fundamental need of matching mental images with reality. *Wealth* may be an end in itself to a certain low type of mind, but for most seekers after gold its value lies in the power it confers on the possessor to fulfill his dreams of ownership and travel and homage and security. *Freedom* is prized not because of any mere sentiment for a word but because it gives largest opportunity for the objectification of the cherished inner thought. In a hospital an artisan, who found for the first time in his life an opportunity to do work in artistic handicraft which he loves, was asked by the superintendent whether or no he would be willing to leave the hospital and go back to the factory again. The patient replied, "I'd like to stay here forever, if only I wasn't a prisoner." Even the chance to do one thing which he was very fond of doing could not atone for the loss of the larger privilege which a free man has of converting endless fancies into facts. *Play* was once defined by one of my teachers in philosophy as anything which one does just because he likes to do it—something which is enjoyed because of what it is in itself, whether it has any further use, makes any contribution to a remote end or not. But why does one like to play golf for example? To a man like Edward Howard Griggs it is a mystery beyond all penetration that any person of sound mind, instead of revelling in the beauty of earth and sky, the sunlight dancing on the leaves, the flight of birds across the blue, should chase up and down a field trying to hit a little white ball and then to find it again after one has hit it, eyes glued on the ground, face set, nerves tense, temper variable, in the grip of a fear that the other fellow will get to the green and the cup with less strokes than oneself. There are no doubt several explanations for this curious social phenomenon, but certainly a large place must be given to the satisfaction of matching mental images with reality. The mental images are many; hitting something, hitting it hard, hitting it straight, belonging, doing what others do, getting exercise, wearing plus-fours! Here is an array of images congenial to the average mind. By the payment of club fees and the dint of practice those images may become realities and in the very becoming satisfy a real mental need. Play is not merely practice in mastery. It is mastery. It is success. In a small way and for a limited time it is a making the world over after the longings of one's heart, bending the stuff of reality to the pattern of desire. *Associations* are not always entered for their own sake but because they promise to lend themselves as instruments for the achievement of some cherished mental aim. Some men become Masons not because they are anxious to learn about the great Architect of the universe but because they thereby gain an ascendancy among their fellows which has seemed to their thinking to possess such a lure. Other men join labor unions because they can thus win a social importance which is denied them by the usual social scorn of mere manual toil. They will strike against their very own interests, strike sometimes when they can without striking get the very thing for which they strike, because for a time the social recognition gained by striking has become a dominant image in their mind. *Work* is satisfying only when it provides the opportunity for the actualization of some cherished mental image. As an experiment an educator hired a man and set him to work in his yard striking a log with the back of an ax; paying him the usual wages. Before noon the man came in and threw up the job and said that he could not work any longer because he had to see the chips fly.[2] The mere impact of the ax head upon a log was not a fulfillment of any mental image which the laborer carried in his mind in connection with both ax and log and his whole self repudiated the farce and would not continue though he was paid for it and needed the money. The nausea at routine which most of us feel comes because that routine is not at all the realization of any satisfying idea. And the thrill which creative labor possesses is just that it is the successful transformation of an ideal conception into concrete existence. An anonymous writer has recently taken a fling at the doctrine of self-expression in an article on "The Refuge of the Impersonal."[3] He declares that a good table is one which is made, not by a man who is seeking to express himself, but by one who has submitted himself to the nature of the wood and to certain principles of carpentry; that the great poet is not a man who has expressed himself but one who has transcended himself; that King Lear is more perfect and sublime than Shakespeare; and the "Ode to a Nightingale" a more flawless creation than its creator. But confession is made that "the desire to write a poem or to fashion a strain of music into a symphony is in part a desire to express oneself," that is to put outside oneself something that first was within. And while insisting that there is present the motive of expressing or fashioning a something felt to be intrinsically excellent, he nevertheless admits that that something which possessed the aspect of the awesome and seemed to come as a divine stranger, nevertheless lay within the mind, was felt in the most personal private recesses of consciousness. Which confession puts the case back into our hands, recognizes the essence of what we are trying to say, namely, that the joy of creative labor of any kind, whether it be the fashioning of a tool, or the writing of a poem, or the production of a symphony, or the inauguration of a new society, is in large part the joy which arises in the successful embodiment of a mental image in external reality.

II

Here dawns problem and tragedy. Life does not lend itself readily to such an embodiment. Circumstances, competition, the intractable character of things and of society, human awkwardness, the conflict between mental images so that the fulfillment of one means the frustration of another—all of these defy the efforts of men and women to give to dreams "a local habitation and a name." Every Sunday the preacher looks out over a congregation of men and women who are in the throes of some defeat; "mute inglorious Miltons" in whose breast the struggle for a mere livelihood has choked the poem that craved to be born; technicians whose knowledge and skill are prisoners of a competitive society which can offer them no positions where the creations of the mind may be wrought into brick and stone and steel; dreamers who are mocked by the stubborn nature of the individuals and of the groups whose co-operation must be given if dreams are ever to be more than dreams; bunglers who have ideas of whose validity there can be little question but who are like the man who has all the parts of a watch before him on the table but just cannot get them all back into the case so that they will function as a whole and keep time, or like a violinist who has a good instrument and knows the location of all the notes and can read music but lacks the final something which can make the violin sob and sigh and sing, or like the speaker who has truth and command of language and a picture of what he would like to have happen to the audience but somehow it never happens. Beside these is a great company who in matching one image with reality must mutilate others just as beloved, who in being true to others must be false to themselves, in discharging public duties must neglect self-culture, in seeking knowledge must "give up the prospects of ever getting an answer to ninety-nine of the puzzles about the world and men . . . in order to stand even a faint chance of solving the hundredth;"[4] who if they are to become scholars must sacrifice love and friendship and hospitality, for "intellectual work taken seriously is a tyrant that grudges nothing more than the ample periods of bodily and mental leisure that are required in order fully to know or to love those about us;"[5] who in being benevolent to some must be cruel to others. There is not now, nor is there any prospect of, a society where men and women can be either consistently loyal to their ideals or consistently successful in the fulfillment of them. Accepting one they must ignore the others. Success in one direction means failure elsewhere.

Out of this simple, self-evident fact arises a great challenge to all who are concerned with the development of personality. In it lies the explanation of many dwarfed and twisted lives. In the light of it must be wrought the strategy which will be effective in the achievement of well-balanced maturity. One of our old hymns asks: "Is this vile world a friend to grace to help me on to God?" Accepted as it is, permitted to do what it will, it is not! The frustrate ghosts about us are the proof. Overcome, mastered, compelled in spite of itself to become the stage whereon the self enacts its Pilgrim's Progress, the world may become the theater of soul making. But it all depends. And much of that contingency arises in connection with the difficulty of matching mental images with reality.

Failure to do so often inspires destructive reactions. Some surrender quickly to the brutal denial which the world makes, and try to bury their mental images out of sight. There results what some psychologists call a repression, concerning whose ultimate explanation there is considerable difference of opinion, but of whose disastrous consequences there can be little doubt. Mental images which have made their appeal cannot be disposed of in that fashion. They refuse to be exiled to some Devil's Island of the spirit. They persist in that unknown somewhere which some call the unconscious mind, but which others like Professor Brightman, refusing to believe the self ever exists in unconsciousness, call the immediate environment of the self; and from there they play havoc with health and with the outlooks and attitudes and judgments and decisions of the conscious self. Current literature is so full of illustrations that it is scarcely necessary to do any more than refer to them—phobias, obsessions, inhibitions, hysterias, which affect otherwise normal people and make them a torment to themselves and a menace to society. Here is a business man long haunted with fear. He is afraid that he will be wrecked on his way to his office, afraid that someone will shoot him down while he is at his desk, afraid to leave his office at night for fear that the records of the day have not been properly kept. He lives the life of a tortured worm. Examination finally discovers that at one time there had come to his mind an image which strongly appealed to one side of his nature but which could not be translated into action without loss of social standing. Frightened by it he did not know what else to do but to try to disown it. But it refused to be disowned. Instead, it took possession of him, ruling his life by the very fear it awakened, leaving him not a master but a slave.

Others accept the defeat of prized mental images and make that defeat the comrade of their days and nights, saturating their lives with its gloom, acquiring persistent moods of inferiority, easily discouraged, always contrasting themselves with others to their own disparagement, full of self-pity, sensitive to slight, self-conscious, self-critical, self-tormenting, incapable of hearty laughter or heroic labor. They drag through life accepting minor assignments, refusing difficult tasks, missing glorious opportunities, submerged personalities! If something could only happen to them once to make them say, "I can," to break the spell of defeat, to help them to turn hopefully to the entertainment of significant images in the effort to actualize them, one is sure that there would be a splendid story to write. But so often that does not happen, and the years come and go in drab succession, their paralyses becoming more and more incurable. In one of my parishes was one who for years carried a mental picture of a career on the concert stage. Before that picture she lighted the candles of her hope, to it she made almost hourly obeisance, for it she toiled incredibly. Then one brutal day her teacher told her that she had no concert voice, that her picture was the product of self-ignorance and the applause of uncritical and cowardly friends who were afraid to tell her the truth. With ruthless hand he tore the picture from her mental wall, trampled it under his feet and sent her out of the studio in despair. Under the cloud of that despair she lived for years. It palsied her aspiration, corroded her confidence, all but cost her her life, and left her a stifled soul, a household Lulu Bett, a social zero. Defeats like that are a personal and social disaster of the first rank.

Some, scourged by disaster, still cling to the mental image and create satisfactions in the imagination and live with them. They become day-dreamers, air-castle architects. Their bodies are in the world of reality; their minds in the world of phantasy. I know one who greatly loved but whose love was denied fulfillment. Unable to contemplate existence without the presence and comradeship and affection of his beloved, he set her in the fairyland of his vivid imagination, whither, when free from the exhausting demands of business or in the loneliness of the night, he took flight and found escape from the hard world of reality. Frances Wickes, in *The Inner World of Childhood,* cites instance after instance of children who created imaginary playmates to satisfy needs and longings which home or playground denied. In milder cases little harm may be done. We are all dreamers on occasion. But too much resort to phantasy may create a distaste for reality, apathy toward relationships with real people, indifference to the demands of one's position, incapacity to distinguish between fact and fancy, a self-absorption which is ruinous.

Others compensate for shattered mental images by Bohemianisms of body or mind. They must have some kind of success, some harmony between conception and execution. They appeal from Phillip sober to Phillip drunk; from brains which are difficult to acquire to beauty which the parlors offer at two dollars a treatment; from ideas which cannot find a hearing to loud voices which ride down all contiguous conversation; from personal achievements which are beyond them to a parade of ancestors which are theirs by the accident of birth. Of Lord Curzon, Viceroy of India, a biographer writes, "The Indian task was colossal and he would have sunk beneath it had he not continually remembered that he himself was a Colossus. He sated his soul by an occasional gesture of imaginative power."[6] All about us are people who are sating their souls by gestures; gestures of intelligence in the place of real wisdom; gestures of propriety in the place of real character; gestures of courtesy instead of real friendship; gestures of creed and ritual instead of real faith; gestures of bravado in the place of real heroism. And gestures never make persons. They may be beautiful symbols of reality. They are hideous substitutes.

One cannot forget the rebels who, finding the world in conflict with mental images, perhaps defeated, refuse to accept defeat but spend their lives in bold, sometimes magnificent, schemes to make their dreams come true; who fling caution to the winds and fling themselves against the gods; who in the deserts of high finance and the jungles of business carry on their adventures; who become "Robber Barons," the Napoleons of Wall Street, the Attilas of Washington, the Casanovas of Newport, the Isadora Duncans of the theater. They match mental images with reality in a spectacular way but they mar reality and make of themselves monsters over which the angels and ultimately themselves must weep.

Finally, there are those who make a piety of renunciation. Feuchtwanger, in the Fifth Book of *Power,* writes: "From the Occident there beats a wild continuous wave upon the land of Canaan, a thirst for life and personality, a will for action, for happiness, for power. . . . But in the south, under the pointed pyramids there lie dead kings embalmed in gold and spices, refusing majestically to give their bodies to destruction, and a wild continuous wave beats from the south upon the land of Canaan, a passionate cleaving to being, a burning desire . . . not to lose the body, not to disintegrate. But from the east there comes a message of gentle wisdom; sleep is better than waking, to be dead better than to be alive; surrender to annihilation . . . renunciation. . . . And many a one follows the road to the very end; from the wild turmoil of doing, from power, happiness and possessions, through a stubborn refusal to renounce, into the bliss of vacancy and absolution, into the ebbtide of inaction and abnegation."[7] One can always do that. It is the easy way. It has been called the Christian way. The Christian summons to action has been translated as an order to inaction. Jesus' call to devotion has been read as a renunciation.

> "Perish every fond ambition,
> All I've sought, and hoped, and known;
> Yet how rich is my condition,
> God and heaven are still my own!"

There is meaning there but not the meaning that has often been read into it, obedience to which has completely devitalized the personality of the misguided.

III

If failure to match mental images with reality

inspires destructive reactions, success with right mental images is the secret for which our quest is being conducted. It means psychic health, the ability to deal with reality, confidence, verve—personality.

Has Jesus any wisdom for us here? Not the conventional Jesus perhaps! If our century holds a Christian spirit anywhere, it is that which animates the life of C. F. Andrews, missionary, friend of Gandhi and Tagore and of India's millions, trusted representative of the British government, author. In *What I Owe to Christ* he declares his conviction about Jesus in unequivocal language. "The grotesquely, distorted portrait of Christ showing us one who was almost insufferably pious, cautiously religious, and conservatively moral, has to be frankly rejected; it is not history."[8] If we of the twentieth century are to find any help for ourselves, we too must turn away from the insufferably pious, cautiously religious, and conservatively moral Jesus, to the real Jesus of history. In him was life and that life is still the light of men, light for us whose world baffles our efforts to match mental images with reality.

He will seem much nearer to us and more pertinent to our need if it is recognized that he had mental images which were not worthy to be embodied in deed. His mind was not a divinely guarded, selective mirror which caught only reflections of the perfect will of God. It was exposed to all the pomp and pageantry, the passing shows and fleeting vanities of the world. It was amenable to the suggestions which find lodgment in all normal minds and out of those suggestions were woven on the loom of desire patterns of conduct which urged to be accepted. He did not have the simple task of receiving from heaven perfect ideas and giving them some worthy expression in action. His was a normal, human consciousness and subjected to the same sort of treatment from bodily desire and social allurement which makes trouble for us. He was tempted, powerfully so! The temptations were not a mere fleeting suggestion, the brushing of the wings of vague desire against the cheek of a virgin conscience. They laid hold upon his imagination, made bold, clearly outlined, vivid pictures in his mind. Recall the story:

And when the tempter came to him, he said, If thou be the Son of God, command that these stones be made bread. But he answered and said, It is written, Man shall not live by bread alone, but by every word that proceedeth out of the mouth of God. Then the devil taketh him up into the holy city, and setteth him on a pinnacle of the temple, and saith unto him, If thou be the Son of God, cast thyself down: for it is written, He shall give his angels charge concerning thee; and in their hands they shall bear thee up, lest at any time thou dash thy foot against a stone. Jesus said unto him, It is written again, Thou shalt not tempt the Lord thy God. Again, the devil taketh him up into an exceeding high mountain, and showeth him all the kingdoms of the world, and the glory of them; and saith unto him, All these things will I give thee, if thou wilt fall down and worship me. Then saith Jesus unto him, Get thee hence, Satan: for it is written, Thou shalt worship the Lord thy God, and him only shalt thou serve.

How did those stories get into the record? No one was there in the lonely place but Jesus. Jesus must have related the struggle of those days to his friends. And when he related them he did not prosaically say, "When I was in the wilderness, the suggestion came to me to try to allay my hunger by a miracle; to win the hearts of the people by some spectacular deed; to conquer by compromise;" rather did he draw three brilliant etchings, with the swift strokes of a master hand, of the pictures which had arisen in his own mind as he contemplated his career and made those crucial decisions which became for him and for us destiny. On at least two other occasions of which we have record, the struggle with ignoble mental images was thrust upon him; once when one of his best friends suggested to him an easier road for his feet to travel than the one which finally led to Calvary; the other when in Gethsemane's darkness, beneath the moaning and wind-swept olive trees, he saw death's grim face peering through the shadows and cried aloud for escape. Remembering that in the Gospels we have only a fragmentary tale, that what we see there is an occasional glimpse of a busy life, these few, brief recitals of temptation reveal to us a man who felt the poignant assault of the mental image of forbidden action.

Jesus knew too what it was to have a mind alive with ideas and ideals to which his world was hostile and to which that world refused the semblance of reality. He had a dream for his mother and his brothers and his sisters, but they did not share it. The words which Matthew puts on the lips of Jesus, "A man's foes shall be they of his own household," sound very like the cry of a heart frustrate in its own domicile. He had a dream for the people of his home town, but they trampled it in the dust and tried to pitch him headlong down the steep hill just outside the village. As far as we know, the town where he grew up, the neighbors who watched him during the silent years, furnished him not a single follower. Only one who has lived long in the same community and formed close ties in work and in play with those whom he has seen almost every day in shop or field or street, sharing with them the experiences of joy and sorrow, of home building and home wrecking, weddings and funerals, holy days and holidays—only such an one can understand the pang and the puzzle which the refusal of his neighbors meant to a friendly heart like Jesus. Much that he wanted to do for his disciples he could not do. He had a vision of a band of prophets; he found them a group of plodders, misunderstanding his words, insensitive to his deepest feelings, thinking in terms of bread and honors when he wanted them to think of the beauty of holiness. Once at least his choking sense of disappointment broke out into words: "Oh foolish generation! How long shall I be with you? How long shall I suffer you?" Just before the end he was talking to them about the persecution which was so soon to befall them and he said, "When I sent you out without purse, and scrip, and shoes, lacked ye anything? . . . But now, he that hath a purse, let him take it, and likewise his scrip: and he that hath no sword, let him sell his garment, and buy one." Prosaic and unseeing as ever they said unto him, "Lord, behold, here are two swords." And he said unto them in despair, "It is enough"—a gesture of most poignant disappointment that, after all these months, they should so utterly mistake his meaning as to assume that he could ever recommend a sword as a means of achieving his purposes. A few hours after that they all took to their heels and left him utterly alone with the soldiers and the mob, and when he stood in Pilate's judgment seat, not a friendly face could be seen in the crowd, not a friendly voice was lifted in his behalf. The men for whom he dreamed and prayed and into whose minds he poured wisdom fit for the ages, had collapsed and failed him utterly.

Historical research has convinced some that the great dream of his life was for his nation. He saw them about to forfeit their mission in the world. Some of the leaders were for compromise with Rome and a mingling of cultures and inevitably a syncretism of religions. Others were for armed rebellion in the hope that God would miraculously abet their feeble battalions against the powerful legions of empire. Either course meant ruin. Compromise and syncretism would water down the rich moral and religious heritage of the prophets until the diluted remnant could provide neither an antiseptic against evil nor nourishment of the good life. Rebellion meant inevitable destruction. They that take the sword always perish by the sword if not physically, at least in all the higher reaches of life. So he flung himself against their threatened madness. He envisioned a nation learning to forgive its enemies, conquering by love, preserving its moral and spiritual heritage behind a bulwark of self-sacrifice. But his last week in Jerusalem mocked that vision and left him standing on the road toward Bethany as it wound around the hill, looking back on the city, and saying, "O Jerusalem, how often would I . . . , but ye would not." It was the heart-break of a devastated dream.

It must not be forgotten that Jesus had some significant mental images which he was able to match with reality in a way so unique as to fill our hearts with sublime envy. Whether or not he actually used the language ascribed to him by John, "I have overcome the world," the words truly describe some bewildering achievements. The chronicle of his defeats, whose significance must not be lost from view, was rivaled by a record of victories. He did have a strange power over people. When soldiers were sent to the Church of Saint Theonas to arrest Athanasius, he tells in his *apologia pro fuga* that he passed out through the midst of them and no one dared to lay hands upon him. Jesus possessed something in his person that made it possible for him to do the same thing with the infuriated crowd of his fellow townsmen. Even in Gethsemane soldiers hesitated to lay hands on him.

He wanted people to be well and strong. The white skin of the leper, the helpless limbs of the palsied, the pitiful gropings of the blind tugged at his heart strings. Modern psychology seems to have found a clue to at least some of the reported cures of the New Testament, so that there is less skepticism about the healings of Jesus than there used to be and considerable more willingness to accept history as history. But whatever the explanation, Jesus undoubtedly had mental images of health for the sick and more than once matched the image with reality.

He craved effective speech and he won it. He said things which made a home for themselves not only in the minds of his closest friends but in the heart of the world. Men cannot forget them. They have tried hard enough. They have buried his words beneath sacraments and liturgies; have submerged them in orthodoxies and heterodoxies; have smothered them in exegetical sophistry and in pagan practice. But they persist in arising from the grave and shaking off the dust and walking the streets and lanes of city and country and halting men in their smug complacencies and sensual rebellions and social selfishness, just when they think they are safest from disturbing challenge. What would we not give to speak so unforgettably and truly?

And he lived. He thought what it would be to be a true son of God. No nobler mental image than that could ever enter the mind. Most of us are content with something very much less. Could we be sons of Socrates or Shakespeare or Beethoven or Lincoln, we should count ourselves blessed among mortals. Could we create or think or act in our time as they did in theirs how rich life would be! But evidently from earliest childhood Jesus had but one mental image for himself—that he should think and act and love like a son of God. How well he succeeded in giving that picture actuality we need not pause to relate. Without the slightest evidence of pose or straining after effect, without a sign of the theatricality of one who is playing a rôle, he talked and lived in such fashion that this critical twentieth century does not bother to ask whether Jesus was like God, but in a bold leap of desire and faith expresses a hope and a conviction that God is like Jesus.

This was the Jesus of history—a Jesus who had some mental images which were unworthy to be matched with reality; others to which the world refused even the semblance of reality; others which he was able to match with reality in a thrilling way. What did he do with the unworthy and the frustrated images? How did he succeed where we have failed? Is there in his strategy a saving word for us who are in the ministry who to-day seek for ourselves and for others, health and maturity of personality?

IV

He did not attempt to disown the unworthy images which succeeded in setting themselves up in his mind and making an appeal to his heart. He must have told them, else his disciples would never have known about them. And they were not pleasant to relate. It could not have been easy for one who lived on so high a plane and had such a momentous sense of mission to confess that it ever occurred to him to try to turn stones into bread or to make a spectacular, crowd-arresting leap from the pinnacle of the Temple or to bow down to Satan. But Jesus admitted it all to his friends and of course to himself. It would be difficult to think of a fact more significant to morals than that. The thing which differentiates the healthy personality from the sick is not that the one is a screen whereon only noble pictures ever make their appearance while the other seems to have no censorship and no restrictions, but, rather, that the one has dealt openly and frankly with the baser sort of images when they have arrived while the other has been shocked by them, has tried to pretend that they did not arrive, has thrust them out of conscious recognition and therefore out of the realm where they could be wisely dealt with. About many things clinical psychologists will not agree, but they are unanimous in their judgment, derived from long experience with all sorts of sick folks, that unwillingness to admit to oneself that one has really been tempted, that ignoble images have ever appeared and made an appeal is at the root of serious personal disorders; and that willingness to confess to oneself and on occasion to others that one has not only thought evil but desired evil, is the beginning of wisdom. Because we are human, evil suggestions will come, will dramatize their delights in the mind, will make their strong appeal. Could men only escape a sense of disgrace over their heritage and learn to meet all that is incidental to it with minds free from the muddying influence of shame, the world would be less frequently the scene of personal disintegration. The historic Jesus is of great significance here. He has been often so unhistorically presented as to discourage men and drive them to play hide-and-seek with the inner reality of their own lives. He has been exalted as the ideal but as an ideal which had no inner struggle, an ideal so antiseptic that even the thought of evil perished on the threshold of his mind. And men and women who attend the sermon, conscious that more than once the thought of evil has crossed the threshold of their minds and entered into an argument which all but convinced them, have gone away disheartened, have gone away feeling that to be his disciples they must be free from all thought and desire that are not holy, have gone away to disown the thought and desire which inevitably come, to be false to reality and to make themselves the victims of unreality in the shape of the fears and sickness and inhibitions and hysterias and weaknesses which repressions insure. A better understanding of Jesus would make an end of that tragedy. In him we see the world's best compelled again and again to entertain temporarily in his mind images of the worst and to deal with them. He did not ignore. He did not deny. And he was not shocked! He did not succumb either. But his victory was wrought in the open, with no sense of shame that he had a fight on his hands. He was as wholesome and poised and yet as drastic as a surgeon when confronted by diseased tissue. He recognized that it was time for action but not for condemnation or concealment or pretense that nothing was there. In such a presence one learns that it is not the coming of an image of evil or the consciousness of its appeal that dishonors him but, rather, what is done about it. And the mind is thus set free to discover what should be done about it.

In that his life is of great significance too. He escaped the thrall of unworthy images and their consequent, insupportable desires not by negation but by affirmation. Over against the tug of the lower and narrower he set the spell of the higher and the more inclusive; over against physical need for bread, the need of the whole nature for God; over against gains to be won by the problematic success of a spectacular deed, the surer gain of obedient faith in spiritual forces; over against any advantage which might accrue to his high crusade by compromise with a lower power, the certainty of values which belong only to homage to the higher. In a real sense he did not wage a war against unworthy images and ignoble desires, he merely summoned other images and desires and let them expel the invader. He knew the hopelessness of a mere struggle against. Though the trouble maker might be banished, the empty house is an invitation to return. Therefore he let the wider appeal of the more inclusive and satisfying end, crowd out what was narrower and ultimately and necessarily disappointing, and so fill the house of life that the others could not find standing room on their return.

Here again is sagacity for those who seek personal fulfillment for themselves and others. "I will not" or "thou shalt not" are of small avail in the presence of appealing images. Only other images with greater fascination are competent for the struggle. And their help is always at hand. For every thought of evil which marshals desire within, there are thoughts of good, which, if they could be summoned, along with a vivid consciousness of the consequences of that good, would in turn marshal stronger desires. In one of the New York papers some time ago appeared an arresting letter from a man who said he had come to New York City to make a fortune and had succeeded to a measurable degree. But after reciting briefly the story of his success he said, "I would give everything I possess if as I look back over the past I could be sure that I had given every man a square deal." If that man could have had at the beginning that knowledge of consequences which the years brought him, the strong aversion which filled him with regret over deeds done would have begotten equally strong resolutions not to do what he did but something else. He would not have felt any impulsion to choose a course which landed him in the gloom where he at last found himself. He did not know or, knowing, did not realize. Realization would have meant regeneration of desire and alteration of deed.

We are, therefore, driven to a recognition of something which our discovery of the place of instinct and emotion has tended to obscure—the function of reason in the making of personality. One cannot reason himself away from an overmastering desire, but he can use reason to survey possible modes of action and to discover consequences. If his reasoning be inclusive enough, it will discover those greater ends whose achievement will mean the greater good, the greater satisfaction of the whole self. And if with that discovery, imagination is called into play to make a vivid image of the greater satisfaction, the lower images will be thrust aside and the stage will be set for action which will make rather than mar the personality. As Canon Grensted says, "Where the heart does not leap the mind has not done its work."[9] There is no hope for the man who will not think. He is doomed at the start to be the victim of transient desires and to lose his very life amid an anarchy of emotional conflict. But for him who will use reason to discover the demands of his total self and the relation of any mental image to those demands, life offers the prospect of continuous fulfillment.

It is at this point that the educative ministry of preaching and teaching can discharge a very important function. Preacher and teacher should be fact finders and fact revealers, should indulge less in denunciation and more in illumination, should say less often or not at all "Don't," and always, "This, and this, and this, will be the result of such a course of action." Jesus did not imply that we are to be scourges to lash people for their misdeeds, but candles to give them light upon the significance of their deeds, to help them to see that virtue is not a fetter but a wing, that goodness is not a crust but a banquet for the whole self; to let no lesson or sermon end until the hearers have had new facts which will make more real to them the belittling, dwarfing results which follow certain modes of conduct and the enlarging, liberating consequences of others; and thus to put within their possession material out of which to build nobler images in their minds when the lesser are inserting themselves and awakening desire. The only kind of teaching and preaching that counts is the kind that unveils life. Less exhortation and more revelation are needed if men and women are to be able to meet temptation as Jesus met it, to answer every alluring suggestion with one still more alluring because it is more sure and inclusive and permanent.

Also here is very clearly seen the function of moral fellowship with Jesus. As one reads his words and ponders his life, new and attractive images arise in the mind, before which others flee like owls and bats at the coming of day. I once had to deal with a man whose heart was hot with revenge. He had been greatly wronged, and because of the injury inflicted so unjustly was preparing to take his family and leave the church. His going would have been a disaster not only to himself and his family but to the church, for he had many friends who would have followed him out of the fellowship and thus would have disrupted an enterprise which at that hour was in a precarious position. I tried every argument to induce him to change his mind and reconsider his withdrawal from membership in the church, but nothing that I said was able to change his temper. He wanted revenge and he knew no better way in which to get it. At last in my desperation I bethought me of Jesus and his cross. I reminded the man that Jesus had also suffered unjustly an infamy far greater than any which was then under consideration. I told him, simply, how Jesus, hanging in pain on the cross, nevertheless looked down even upon the men who had driven the nails through his hands and feet and with a heart full of compassion prayed, "Father, forgive them, for they know not what they do." I told him that here was a great opportunity for him to show that the spirit of Christ had not departed from the sons of men and that that spirit could enable one who had been injured to forgive those who had so greatly wronged him. I appealed to him to come back to the church and to continue his labors there for the sake of Christ. I had scarcely dared to look at him during this final appeal but when at the close I turned my eyes in his direction I saw that his head was bowed and that the tears were stealing down his cheeks. I knew that victory was won. The strange fascination of the man upon the cross had driven out the image of revenge which had taken the throne of that man's mind and heart and in its stead had enthroned the spirit of forgiveness and love. That man returned to his place in the sanctuary and in the active membership of the church. The church was saved from dissolution and the kingdom of God moved on to new triumphs in the community.

Jesus is of great value to those who have been fascinated by noble mental images but have found their world intractable and defeating. He met his defeats as wholesomely as he met his temptations. He did not succumb to gloom, become self-conscious, self-critical, self-despairing, but continued radiant, wholesome, confident. He never ceased trying. When Peter wavered and denied, he kept on praying and hoping for him. When he saw Judas tottering toward the abyss of treachery, he threw his arms about him in an effort to pull him back. Though the mad nationalism of the leaders of the people seemed to have neither wit nor conscience, he went to Jerusalem the very last week of his life in a bold effort to challenge the nation to accept his leadership and come back to their senses and to God. And even when he saw he must suffer and die, he did not despair. He believed in God. He accepted his sufferings and death as a part of the divine strategy. Faith triumphed over experience. He became reconciled to postponements. He committed his dreams and defeats to the unconquerable God and thus escaped the paralysis of defeat and retained the inspiration of his dreams to the very end. Following his example men will neither succumb to defeat nor take refuge in phantasy.

They will face the real world and cling to their ideals; they will cling to their ideals and face the real world. The gods of the old mythology were gods of escape. But there is no suggestion of escape in Jesus. His followers have sometimes used him so. "I left it all with Jesus long ago." "Jesus paid it all." "Let me to thy bosom fly." There is truth which may be read into those words but there is also error which has been associated with them, principally the error of making Jesus a means of escape from life. The real Jesus "did not free his followers from the hardships of living or from the pains of dying. He showed men that life was something from which they could not escape by some trick of faith but was a challenge to be met. He showed them a fullness, a significance in living which only those who faced that challenge could ever understand."[10] They who catch his spirit may often be defeated but they are never vanquished, for they have a faith that overcomes the world as he had, a faith that keeps on hoping and striving to the very end, and when it falls on sleep commits not merely its spirit but its cause into the Father's hands. Hartley Burr Alexander in his noble contribution to *Contemporary American Philosophy,* wrote, "When I watched at my accustomed post which is far out over the ramparts, full conscious of the gulfs of chaos, my courage is little from myself and much from a sign upreared on a hill loftier than the Acropolis from whence comes not the wisdom of the Greeks but the hope of all mankind."[11] Father Tyrrell has confessed for all who have lived in any real spiritual fellowship with Jesus, "Often I have been tempted to run away from my work, but always the strange figure of that man upon the cross sends me back again."

Finally, in Jesus is the secret of the realization of many dreams which have baffled us, dreams of usefulness, of power in our relation to people, of victory over the temptations of life, and of a character more like that of God. Supremely his was a life of obedience to and fellowship with God. Our weakness is largely the result of our wilfulness; our powerlessness is the outcome of our prayerlessness. Surrender in contests with men is hailed as a bit unmanly; surrender in our relations with God is the only road to mature manhood. Tennyson knew it:

> "Our wills are ours, we know not how,
> Our wills are ours to make them thine."

General Booth knew it when in answer to one who asked him the secret of his useful life, replied, "I determined to let God have all there was of me." Surrender means the opening of life-starved souls to the infinite life; the turning of our untutored ignorance to the wisdom which comes from above; the yielding of our narrow and feeble affections to a love more boundless than the sea. It is the testimony of life that the more completely we surrender ourselves the more truly do we become ourselves. Surrender does not mean bondage but release. It does not devitalize but invigorates. In surrender only can occur what religion describes as conversion but what the psychologist calls a process by which a self consciously divided, inferior, unhappy, becomes consciously united, superior, and happy. In surrender only are the channels open between man and God, so that prayer becomes not a begging of gifts but fellowship and a fellowship which witnesses an increasing illumination and transformation of the self until it approximates that of Jesus.

CHAPTER VI

PERSONALITY AND SELF-RESPECT

BEFORE James A. Garfield became President of the United States he served for a number of years in Congress as representative of an Ohio district. One day as he reviewed his political career, he said to some friends: "I have for many years represented a district in Congress whose approbation I greatly desired; but, though it may seem a little egotistical to say it, I desired still more the approbation of one person, and his name is Garfield. He is the only man I am compelled to sleep with and eat with and live with and die with; and if I do not have his approbation I should have bad companionship." Of all the demands of the self as it moves toward the achievement of personality, there is none more urgent than the demand for self-respect, none of which the self is more conscious, none to which its complex activities bear more striking witness. Men find it difficult sometimes to believe in themselves but cannot escape the necessity of doing it.

They often neglect duty; under the pressure of some strident real flout their ideals, play the coward instead of the hero, speak or act a lie rather than the truth, stoop to the little instead of rising to the great, give way to an excess which mocks their intention of self-control, are swayed from the path of justice and fair play. But only under great constraint do they confess to themselves the low quality of their performance, for such confession assails that estimate of themselves to which they passionately cling. One lad, who had boasted to his mother of his courage with the solemn assurance that he would not run from anything, encountered a huge mastiff on the sidewalk in front of his home one day and promptly took to his heels. When he reached the asylum of the house, his mother, who had watched the whole episode, said to him teasingly, "I thought you said you were not afraid of anything." "Oh, I am not," he replied. "I just thought it was a good time to see how fast I could run." Running *from* was not compatible with his ideal for himself; running *fast* was. So, of course, he was merely running fast. His interpretation was thoroughly human. Men are forever interpreting their actions so. Cowardice is merely discretion; falsehood is loyalty to a larger reality than the immediate situation; littleness is simply the hot defense of some value which others have considered beneath their notice; excess is only escape from the humdrum of life; apparent injustice is merely the fortune of the game. And these glorifications of meanness are not so much an attempt to deceive others as to enable them to maintain their own good opinions of themselves. Men sometimes sink very low in the moral and social scale but seldom so low that the need of self-respect is not strikingly present. If they measured themselves by our standards, their self-respect would be shattered, so they set up standards of their own, standards of gang loyalty or of desperate daring, standards which even in their low estate they can fulfill and in the fulfillment of which they preserve their own sense of worth. A man with a long prison record came to see me. He was no ordinary crook. He was a desperado. As he told me his story of bank robbery and prison sentence, with untellable violence, whatever regret and shame appeared was more than covered by his feeling of superiority as he contrasted his career with that of house burglars, "porch climbers" he contemptuously called them, who enter homes while people are defenseless in sleep and make away with petty values. His supreme achievement in self-respect came when he descanted upon the depravity of men to whom he applied the epithet "rats," who "squealed," betrayed their comrades by turning state's evidence. He was the most antisocial character I have ever met. But even he had to assure me and himself that there was an essential respectability about him and his career. Utter condemnation he would not accept for a moment.

Criticism which, if intelligent, is a most valuable contribution to the making of a good life, is nevertheless one of the things which it is most difficult to receive intelligently and thankfully. Usually it is resented. Men afterward may go and make the changes which the critic has suggested, but it is difficult to admit that he is justified in his criticism, because if he is correct, the criticized are wrong, their judgment mistaken, their execution faulty; they are less the man or the artist than they like to think they are. Criticism is always a bit humiliating. Humility may be praised as a virtue but humiliation is abhorred as an experience. It puts us a notch lower than our own humility is willing to accept. One of the most gracious spirits in the American pulpit was greeted after the morning sermon with the comment of one of his congregation, "Well, doctor, you gave us husks this morning." Stung to the quick, this guileless, gracious soul flushed and hotly replied, "Yes, and the swine were all here to eat them." We all need to be told at times that what we have offered as corn has been mere husks, but the very resentment we feel is evidence of our sensitiveness about ourselves and our labors. We cannot endure to think meanly of either. When criticism becomes ridicule, the hurt becomes torture. "The fear of ridicule is even greater than the fear of physical injury, for ridicule attacks our feeling of equality in relationships and robs us of our personal dignity and competence."[1] Miss Kingsley, relating her experience with West Africans, said that she could chaff and ridicule them into doing things that others could not make them do with a club. Even a savage must respect himself, is more quickly moved to action by threats against his self-respect than by brute force. President Wilson, assailed by denunciations which impeached his integrity and wisdom, wrote, "It is just as hard to do your duty when men are sneering at you as when they are shooting at you." The impulse to preservation, when not compelled to defend the physical self must defend the psychic self, the destruction of which is more terrible than death. In one of the cities of America the mayor was removed from office by action of the governor. His safety director was tried on charges of conspiracy against the common weal and was sentenced to the penitentiary. The trail of the serpent which wound in and out of City Hall stood revealed and brought down upon officeholders the wrath and condemnation of the public. But within a few years the man who had been removed from the mayoralty was again a candidate. He could not live with himself as long as in the judgment of citizens he was unfit to live with them. He sought office not for salary but only because by election and vindication could he retrieve his forfeited self-respect. His nerve seemed colossal but it was only another evidence of the imperious demand of the self, of any self, for a sense of its own worth.

One is embarrassed by the wealth of material illustrative of the large place which this demand occupies in human life. Men like the books and sermons which confirm their beliefs, not merely because the beliefs themselves are comforting or inspiring, but because a confirmation of that to which they have surrendered minds and hearts is a commendation of their judgment and an approval of their sense of values. People are fond of histories which prove that America never fought an unjust war, never lost any war, never was outwitted at a peace table. They have a voracious appetite for the oratory which spins a halo of rhetorical splendor about America's manifest destiny, about the impeccable wisdom of the founding fathers, about the unimpeachable glories of the Constitution, about the inexhaustible strength of America's resources, because forsooth are they not Americans and do they not share the grandeur which characterizes everything which comes to birth on our shores! On the other hand they enjoy the biting satires of a

Mencken, the debunking biography of a Rupert Hughes, the derision of a Ben Hecht, the burlesque "Of Thee I Sing," because anything which enables them to snicker at anyone else fills them with a satisfying sense of their own superiority. One very large element in humor is its answer to man's need for self assurance. Sometimes we laugh with others; sometimes we laugh at them. And when we laugh at them we laud ourselves. "What fools these mortals be!" we say aloud with Shakespeare; "What wise men we are!" is the antiphonal in our own hearts. So deep is the demand for self-respect that psychologists who believe in and recommend sublimation as the only process "given under heaven or among men whereby men must be saved," recognize that no sublimation is possible which does not reckon with it. "The characteristics of a perfect sublimation are three in number. It must be interesting and pleasurable; it must be beneficial to the community; and it must satisfy the man's ideal for himself."[2] There can be no integration of the energies of the self about a task which contradicts one's estimate of himself and his capacities.

The loss of self-respect is always a tragedy. In its first stages it produces a feeling of incapacity. One begins to lose confidence in his power to do or to be. He ceases to dream and to dare. He looks down and not up, in and not out. His nerve declines. A certain vervelessness takes possession of him. He becomes flabby, mentally and morally. He is amenable to low suggestions of all sorts. He ceases to say, "No, I could not do that," in the presence of temptation. He begins to feel that he can, and that he is likely to, and that he might as well. It cannot matter very much if he goes to the dogs. In his own eyes he is actually there. Often this decay of self-respect is accompanied by bitter pangs. Robert Burns put into vivid language what a multitude have felt but lacked the power to express: "Regret! Remorse! Shame! Ye three hell hounds that ever dog my steps and bay at my heels." When regret over what one has done is not counterbalanced by some prideful memories, the end is not far. The devastating misery of one who looks at himself and finds nothing there that his intelligence approves or his moral judgment commends is the prelude to suicide. One cannot live with himself unless he can respect himself in some measure.

II

For this reason the self is ever striving, sometimes frantically, to maintain or to restore self-respect. Because it is untaught or because it is mistaught its efforts are often subversive of the type of personality which is our human goal.

Challenged by its own misdeeds and failures,

instead of acknowledging them and accepting responsibility for them and attempting correction, it can close its eyes to the truth and project its unpleasant emotional accompaniments upon someone else, escaping a sense of condemnation by accusation, despising another instead of itself. It is a commonplace that we often hate those whom we have wronged. It hurts our pride to admit that we have been in the wrong ourselves and so we divert our disapproval. Instead of apology there is further attack.

Confronted by a reality which denies the truth of its opinions or beliefs, the self often preserves its intellectual respectability by a rationalization of reality into conformity with its beliefs. A. A. Milne has dramatized that very common experience in his play, *The Ivory Door*. About that Ivory Door in the king's palace there was a legend that no one who entered it ever came back. He disappeared out of life. For three hundred years that legend was a part of the fixed beliefs of the people. Then one day a king came to the throne who had a passion to know. After a struggle with his own fears he finally put the key in the lock, turned it, opened the door, and passed through. He stumbled through a dark passage and emerged into the sunlight again. But would people believe that it was he who came back? No, indeed, for if it were, then their belief and the beliefs of their ancestors were wrong. That could not be. Though the king stood there before them, it was not he, but a clever impostor who wanted to claim the throne. The evidence of eyes and ears must be denied to save their faces. So the king lost his kingdom. But he understood. And when the queen asked, "Do they want to lose their king," he answered: "No, but rather him than their legend. . . . When I came safely through the door I was telling each one of my people that he was a fool and a coward, a fool to believe and a coward to fear. Could I expect them to cry to the world, 'We are fools and cowards! Long live his Majesty who has proved it to us'?"[3] Many creeds, economic, political, religious, survive even in the presence of contradictory facts because the renunciation of them would be a gentle confession, "We have been fools to believe and cowards to fear." And not only society but the believers and the fearful ones suffer in such a confession. So self-respect is maintained at a fearful cost—the lack of honesty and intelligence and a grasp upon reality.

The passion for a high estimate of oneself often leads to subservience to the judgment of others. One is naturally amenable to the opinions of his fellows. In spite of Kipling, it is difficult to "trust yourself when all men doubt you and make allowance for their doubting too." The brave king in *The Ivory Door* almost ceased to believe in his own identity when people denied it. "Tell me," he says to Brand, his trusted body servant, "tell me, for, indeed, I am beginning to doubt myself now—am I the king?"[4] It is not easy to believe oneself right when many others say he is wrong. And in one's eagerness to think of himself as right one easily becomes subservient to the intellectual and moral judgments of others, forfeits his independence, loses sight of the gleam which may be a star to lead him to some Bethlehem, and so by his very passion to guard himself loses himself.

Men often seek the satisfaction of the need for self-respect by identification with a group, whether it be racial, political, social, or religious. If one shares the glory of the group, then the more glorified the group the greater the luster which results from belonging. Hence come the eulogists of Nordic supremacy like Hitler, who could not give an intelligent definition of a Nordic if asked, and who, if there were a Nordic race, could not belong because he comes of a Mediterranean strain, but who covers his own weakness by an alliance with manufactured Nordic glory. Hence comes the Chauvinist, whose hot and intolerant nationalism is a menace to the peace of the world and to the very existence of his own government, but who in his "my-country-always-right" attitude finds by participation a sense of his own imperishable rightness. Hence comes the denominationalist who achieves personal elevation in reciting the virtues of his own creed and sect. All of them develop attitudes which are alien to that healthy social personality which ought to be the goal of all our striving. They fail to discover in themselves those weaknesses of judgment and affection and will which keep them from the goal because the vicarious respectability they have borrowed from race or country or sect soothes them into self-content.

III

Medieval religion listed pride as one of the seven deadly sins. If pride be self-applause as the result of a non-critical attitude toward its own thoughts and deeds, it is deadly. Nothing is more likely to induce such pride than borrowed glory. But there is a difference between self-applause and self-respect. Self-applause is not only ignorance of the self but of the ideal in the presence of which the self will always be humble. Self-respect is never enough content with itself or its achievements to feel like applauding; but at the same time it is enough aware of the essential worth of its capacities and purposes never to give away to self-denunciation or to self-despair. Self-respect is a consciousness of personal values which, though perhaps as yet embryonic and immature, are worth living with and living for and living out, such living having significance not for the self alone but for society. The value of such an element is almost self-evident. Without it there can be no value. With it all the losses which life can inflict cannot rob life of value. Friends may die, position be forfeited, the world hostile, but as long as self and its destiny remain as objects of worth there will be neither despair nor surrender. Temptation encounters a serious foe in one's sense of his own worth. A young man was standing on a street corner in the company of a frivolous and wild set. An older man of the town who knew him and his family and the hopes which were entertained for him and the young man's own deeper aspirations for himself passed along. Sauntering up to the young man he whispered in his ear, "Don't throw yourself away." That appeal went straight to the heart of the incipient prodigal. He did not want to throw himself away, in spite of his love of conviviality. After a few moments he separated himself from that crowd and never returned. He sought his pleasure elsewhere and saved his life from the contaminations of the "fast" set. When anyone, young or old, has a sense of something in himself too valuable to throw away and recognizes that all that the moral experience of the race agrees to call evil is just throwing oneself away, he has a stimulus to moral discipline whose effectiveness simply cannot be measured. The low judgments of society cannot frighten one from duty or from creativity if he believes in himself enough to believe that his interpretations and his creations are authentic, or that he can be the channel of a revelation of eternal reality. Coventry Patmore made whatever contribution was his because he believed in himself. His Odes were unconventional but he never apologized for them. "He kept the path he had made for himself regardless of public taste or private praise. Prophets do not poll their opinions. He uttered his to the stars. . . . Better be unheard on the heights than to win snuffling acquiescence from the mob below."[5] Every creator has to decide between himself and the mob; will the preacher preach for crowds or for the truth; will the artist paint for the gaudy taste of the multitude, or even for the formal and standardized taste of the critics, or for his own inner testimony to beauty; will the musician write to set heads bobbing and feet dancing or out of loyalty to his own genius? The answer determines destiny, and the answer is determined by the measure of self-respect which is his. The same decision falls upon us humbler folk. Will we be ourselves, hold to our own convictions of duty, our own interpretations of life, our own aims, or shall we be swayed by the convictions and interpretations and aims of our set or the people into whose company life has tossed us? The answer will be determined largely by the reality of our respect for our convictions and interpretations and aims, that is, by our self-respect. The need for self-respect is, therefore, not an artificial want which has succeeded in passing itself off as a need, but it is a real need without whose satisfaction the self will not achieve real personality.

IV

That satisfaction is very difficult these days. A mechanistic philosophy has been trying to persuade the thinker that he is only a conscious microbe crawling over a speck of whirling dust in a universe of dizzy distances, his conceit soon to be answered by oblivion. It is not philosophy but the practical operation of modern life which violently assails the self-respect of multitudes. It gathers them into cities where they are swallowed up in hurrying crowds, no one of whom seems to care whether they live or die. They become anonymous, save to a few; and anonymity makes war on the sense of worth. When nobody stops you on the street to say "Hello," or calls you on the telephone to ask you how you are, or misses you when you are not at church, or invites you to their home, or dreads vacation because it takes them away from you; when you become a mere "hand" or a clerk, or a dweller in the third floor back, or a mere cog in the machine or a cash register from which the landlord collects rent once a month, it isn't easy to keep on believing in your own worth to society or to keep alive a sense of caring very much whether you can go on with yourself. When you have no voice in the determination of hours and wages and working conditions but are victims of an impersonal law of supply and demand or of the brutal manipulations of robber barons; when the employer takes less care of you than he does of the machine at which you work; when you are reduced to the level of a mere pawn in the game of wealth or power; when you read that thirteen millions lost their lives in the recent Great War and that you might have been one of that thirteen millions, and you know that the government which sent you to death would care as little about you as the governments of the world care for anyone of the millions who have gone to dust in the scramble for a place in the sun; when your work offers you no challenge to skill but is something that anybody else with eyes and hands and feet could do just as well and that some day a machine may do a great deal better; when society has nothing for you to do and you become a problem to the world and to your family and to yourself; when, as has happened in the last four years in thousands of cases, you have spent money and time in college and university training, only to discover that it all has created no demand for you and you sit idle year after year, a drain upon the resources of the state and of your friends, it is difficult to maintain a real conviction of personal value. It is one of the strange paradoxes of history that in the very period when some theoretical humanists have exalted man and made him independent of God, society has evolved a condition which has deposed multitudes and reduced them to serfdom to impersonal laws and bestial cunning. The preacher to-day is confronted by many people who need his help to achieve that self-respect which is essential to personal fulfillment. If he cannot help them here, he cannot help them anywhere very much.

Has Jesus anything to offer to us who have such a task imposed upon us and through us to those the very foundations of whose personality are constantly and destructively assailed by a social situation?

Not as he is often preached. His teachings have been distorted until they have become a recommendation of self-negation or self-impeachment. "Blessed are the meek"—a great word to those who understand it, a word which can be obeyed only by one who has such a sense of his own worth that he does not need ever to assert it and cannot be bothered by any denial. But it has been interpreted to mean that one must think so lowly of himself that another's contempt is acceptable confirmation of his own self-depreciation. "If any man come to me and hateth not his life also"—that word has often been read as if one's life were something to be lightly tossed away rather than a great prize to be sacrificed only to a still greater cause. Jesus' whole mission has been described as one of mercy alone, as if God sent him and he gave himself, not because there was anything of worth in us but just because out of sheer goodness of heart he brought that on which man had no claim and which would give value to the valueless. The work of divine grace and love was not to polish a diamond in the rough or to refine gold of its dross but to make diamonds out of dirt, gold out of garbage. The facile interpretation of human destiny which prepared a hell for millions because they had not been baptized in the name of Christ, gave more worth to a rite than to a race. Jesus' own person has been so described as to cast a shadow upon all other persons. Whether he was born of a virgin is a question upon which he never made comment, but it has been argued over and over that only one so born could be of much help to us, an argument which rates very meanly the process by which the rest of us came into the world and by that very fact reduces us to a very low estate. In the effort to understand him men, awed by his splendor, have lost sight of his human nature and have deified him in such absoluteness that you and I have no share in him. He has been presented as a revelation of God, not of man; the disclosure of what God is but not of what man is or may become. He is, therefore, not an inspiring ideal but a discouraging apocalypse. One earnest, thoughtful man read a recent book on Jesus written by a religious leader whose voice has been heard in every city in the United States and many foreign lands, and when he came to those pages where the person of Jesus was described, he wrote on the margin of the page, "The author develops the idea of the uniqueness of Jesus in such a fashion as to fill me with despair."

The Jesus of history never fills anybody with despair. He is the great missioner of self-respect. Mark Rutherford once said that he would like to add one more Beatitude—"Blessed are they who give us back our self-respect." Jesus' whole life was a valiant effort to persuade men to revalue themselves. He came to a people who were enslaved, downtrodden, perpetually subject to the taunts of their Roman conquerors and he began at once to open to them the door of hope. His very first sermon had as its text, "The spirit of the Lord is upon me, for he hath anointed me to preach the gospel to the poor." He told them that they were not accursed but blessed: "Blessed be ye poor." He astounded everybody by his attitude toward the lowliest and the outcast, toward the whole tattered crowd who had ceased to care. None of them had fallen so low but that he treated him with dignity and respect. Read once again his encounter with Zacchæus the tax collector, whom everyone despised; with Mary Magdalene, who had loved not wisely but too well; with a street woman whom her neighbors thought only worth enough stones to kill her; with the five times divorcee who had not even bothered to marry the last man whom she had picked up. If they had been sages and saints, he could not have greeted them more courteously nor dealt with them more deferentially. Hear his characterization of the lost—the lost coin, lost sheep, lost boy; all of them too valuable to be lost, all of them worth a search, all of them the occasion of a jubilee when found. A great deal of unnecessary mystery and of insupportable theology have been woven about his death, but no one can read the records and appraise his purpose with any degree of fairness and not recognize that Jesus believed that he was dying for men, that in some fashion which he did not try to explain, his death would make it possible for men to have and to be what was otherwise impossible. Eliminating all the unworthy ideas associated with the words satisfaction, oblation, atonement, the fact remains crystal clear; as far as will and consecration were concerned Jesus did die for men. Some men have died for the truth; Socrates drank hemlock rather than be false. Others have died for an institution; Nathan Hale, facing the British firing squad, said, "I regret that I have but one life to give to my country." Others have died to vindicate themselves. By death all of them have demonstrated the value they set upon truth or country or self-justification. But Jesus died for men. His death, as his life, was his seal upon the worthfulness of human nature and its unlimited possibilities. His cross, the instrument of his shame, is his testimony to our essential glory. If its meaning be perceived and accepted, man can lift his head and walk abroad. However low he may have fallen, man still has capacity for the heights. However far he may have wandered, there is still a place kept at home for him. However much he may have failed, he is still within reach of a triumph. However near he may be to death, he still has an aptitude for life eternal. That is the judgment of Jesus, and we ought to let men know about it.

His own person is the magna charta of our poor humanity. Men recognize his moral splendor, his spiritual beauty. What we have not helped them to recognize is that his splendor is the splendor of our nature, his beauty is the beauty of a fulfilled human personality. He is the demonstration, before the eyes of centuries, of the rich possibilities of the very human nature which we sometimes despise and of which we even despair. Jesus was a spiritual genius, and not many of us can ever be that. He was a prophet, and prophets arrive only occasionally. He was the Son of God in whom sonship had its most perfect realization. But genius and prophet and Son of God as he was, nevertheless his was a human life. He was "one of ours." He became "man's best man." Because he is our best we must think of God in terms of him. But he is still *our* best. We must believe that he could be our best only because he had the most of God which ever succeeded in pouring itself into a human being. But that most was still poured into a human nature. It reveals man's capacity for God, the extent to which the finite can become the home of the infinite. It declares man to be, not mud constantly being molded by the fingers of childish circumstance and straightway losing its shape in the first summer shower, but marble with a capacity to receive all the artistry of the divine sculptor and to retain it through the ages. A long while ago Job in his misery gathered himself together for a great assertion of faith. "I know that my vindicator liveth, and that some day he shall stand upon the earth." Jesus is the vindicator of Job and of all the rest of us. No one can look at Jesus and ever be in despair about our human heritage. We have the material for the making of personality in ourselves. All that we need is to find a Maker.

Here again we are driven back to Jesus. He not only exhibits a faith in humanity which helps to kindle men's faith in themselves, not only demonstrates on the plane of human life what are the possibilities within us, but he directly gives men an enhanced self to respect. To such an event as this must man always come if the demand for self-respect is to be met. So great a need cannot find a convincing answer in a justification of human nature in general. There is always a possibility that one may be an exception, and most of us have, sooner or later, experiences which make that seem more than a possibility. We are sure. We are only a puzzle to ourselves and a burden to others. Jesus can and does change all that. "If any man be in Christ, he is a new creature," wrote a man of long ago, and all centuries and all classes since have experienced that regeneration of self which has issued in a new and nobler personality. To some it has come quickly by a simple act of surrender and faith, after careful teaching and example which revealed to them the beauty of Jesus and their own ugliness. One lad whom I knew, in the simplicity of his youth gave all that he knew about himself to all that he knew about Jesus and like a flash there came to him a fusing of old scattered aims in one master sentiment and passion, a sense of release from bondage and of new freedom to obey the moral law within, and he described what had happened to him in language as simple as it was revealing, "I feel so new inside." To others what has occurred has been a slow, steady process of living much in spiritual fellowship with Jesus, pondering his words, opening the heart to his vision of life and duty, trying day by day in great crises and in commonplace duties to incarnate his spirit until, without knowing just when it happened, they are aware that they have grown, changed, acquired a certain solidity of character, certain patterns of action, certain high resolves, certain leanings toward truth and beauty and goodness which they can ascribe only to him and which give them a new feeling not only about him but about themselves. But to both groups it has happened that with humility and yet with assurance they write "sons of God" after their names and face all the repudiations of life without a quiver. Yonder is a man whose early life seemed to be a conspiracy against any sense of worth. It assailed him with the shame of poverty, the humiliation of a physical handicap, the consciousness of social awkwardness and moral failure, and the preaching of worm-of-dust, hell-fire theology. But he has grown into a poised manhood which is truly meek and yet masterful, combining in a splendid way the independence which makes for leadership with that dependence upon Another which makes for gentleness. I asked him how it all came about. His answer was, "An experience, mediated through faith in Christ and fellowship with him, gave me standing before God and among the people who seemed to be the best. After that I did not care very much what some individuals and some groups thought about me. Their doubts about me have not disturbed my faith in myself or in Him in whom I believed or in the direction in which I am going. Of course there have been times—for I am human—when I have despised myself, wished I were dead. Yet he makes me feel that there is something here to be respected, fought for, cherished, developed; something that has a right to live, that has a mission; something to share; something that with Him can come through all defeats and despairs to ultimate victory." Jesus does do that if he gets a chance. Are we preaching the kind of a Jesus who does?

CHAPTER VII

PERSONALITY AND COMRADESHIP

"HOMER is not immortal because he observed that the Pleiades do or do not set in the ocean. The greater part of poetry's subject matter is as old as humanity. It is the things which go with hunger and thirst and love and the facing of death."[1] In no other way can the preacher achieve even a relative immortality. It is important that he should know about the Pleiades and about electrons and about the laws of thermodynamics, especially if he feels it necessary to talk about them. One preacher of no mean ability invited the students from a nearby university to attend his services in a body. A respectable number of them came. Had the preacher remained in his own field, they would have listened to him with respect. But he attempted a sermon on "Religion and Science." His science was so faulty that they were sure he knew nothing about that and wondered if he knew anything about religion. When the preacher opens his mouth about anything, he ought to make sure that what he offers as fact is fact. Happily, his ministry does not depend for its depth and richness upon his ability to make wise observations about the stars in the firmament or the stars within the atom. If he, like the poet, can bring good news about "hunger and thirst and love and the facing of death," he will always have a hearing and a blessed human result.

Once the ministry had much to say about the facing of death. That was the "one far off divine event" to which every creature moved. Earth was but a training school; death, the commencement when life really began. To prepare men to die was the consuming purpose for which the preacher lived. In my library is a book of deathbed scenes, the product of a former generation, in which, in as vivid style as the author could command, the death agony of the infidel and the death glory of the believer were set in vivid contrast. The book was written not to satisfy a morbid curiosity but with an evangelistic purpose. Behind it lay a conviction that the way to win men to righteousness was not by a portrayal of noble lives but by the picture of painful deaths. The preacher of yesterday faced death.

Later came a renewed interest in hunger and thirst and a new comprehension of the part that their demand and satisfaction play in the making of personality. The social gospel began to be heard in our churches. It was recognized that it was of little avail to attempt to interest men in the bread of life when they were starving for bread from the bakers; or to offer souls a drink of living water when lips were parched for the lack of a decent supply of drinking water. That simple truth with all its corollaries has not yet dawned upon the minds of many preachers and laymen, and the result is that one Baltimore paper and some bishops and official boards are still exhorting preachers to preach the gospel whenever anyone in the pulpit ventures to offer a gospel for the whole man, body as well as soul, for man the wage-earner or profit-taker as well as the man the worshiper. But the light is slowly permeating the darkness of tradition and of prejudice and of passion, and interpreters of religion are beginning to deal with hunger and thirst.

I

To-day we are to venture into that other realm with which all good poetry and all redemptive preaching must be concerned. It represents a need of the self which is second to none other, but its significance is not recognized often either by the self or by those who are trying to help selves become persons. Archbishop Temple calls it "love." We shall use another word which may help us to face our human situation without the emotional entanglements which the word "love" creates and without the unhappy connotations with which a barnyard literature and an erotic moving-picture industry have surrounded the minds of us all. Instead of love let us talk about comradeship. In so doing we shall be able to keep our feet on the ground, and we shall also be more likely to explore the wide and significant area of human need which confronts us. Comradeship is a more sober word but it is also more sufficient. It has a significance which often does not attach to the more romantic term. If we can discover that significance and help each other to achieve it, we shall have made a real contribution to the realization of personality.

By some, the need of one self for another has been treated as largely a biological phenomenon. They have christened that phenomenon with a word which most of us have come to loathe and have indulged in some curious philosophies about it. They have made its satisfaction the supreme need of life. They have sought to widen the opportunity for satisfaction, to make it socially permissible and individually safe, so that those who cannot marry can mate. They have assumed that the satisfaction of this is the satisfaction of the whole self, and that marriage in itself is the final answer to the clamor within. Verily I say unto you, they have their reward. One of Ludwig Lewisohn's heroines discovered it when, after an adventure, she came to herself and moaned in her disillusionment, "Is that all?" It was all, and it wasn't very much! It can never be the answer to the deep hunger of the self for another. A confusion similar to that which characterizes some of our Philistines affects our Puritans, though it inspires a very different program. Thinking only of comradeship of the body, they have thrust aside the whole experience as of the earth and earthy, have judged it to be a mere matter of appetite, and, like all appetite, a mere accident of our corporeal existence, and have given it neither consideration nor counsel. They have ignored the need for fellowship which is deeper than any mere biological impulse, and which through all biological frustrations and fulfillments remains to plague the self which fails of an answer and to enrich the self if one succeeds in finding the heart that responds unto his own. They therefore have proven inadequate ministers to personality, as must everyone who treats the self as if it were an entity which could grow in comparative isolation or which needs at most the casual, intermittent, superficial contacts of general society.

Others have considered sufficient the comradeship of conviviality. They have thought only of such a sharing of selves as comes when people sit together at the festal board or dance together to thrilling music or contend with each other in games of wit or skill. To be able to say to others,

"We have had good times together," seems to them to exhaust the reasonable demands which our growing selves can make upon any other selves. Playmates are no superfluity in youth or age. They are often a deliverance from unhealthy moods which in isolation easily become a habit and ultimately a vice. The man who faces you on the other side of the net may on occasion do your soul as much good as the man who looks at you from behind the pulpit. His best service may be not in what he does to the ball but in what he does to you. But playmates are not necessarily nor even usually comrades. And when they have departed there is often a strange ache discovered in the heart which one forgets when the festivities are on but which reminds one of its presence the moment the hush comes.

> "Many a heart is aching
> If you could read them all,
> Many a hope has vanished
> After the ball."

So ran a popular song of yesterday and with a surprising amount of truth.

Others have believed that comradeship in work or in a cause furnishes an adequate answer to the demand for an escape from the isolations of the self and for participation in the hopes and dreams and energies of others. They too have emphasized a value. Though it be but the sawing of a log in the depths of a winter forest, if there is a man at the other end of the saw, one is happier and better for his work than if he toiled at a task which required no understanding of and no co-ordination with another's purpose and action. And when a piece of work becomes a crusade, requiring a shared idealogy and demanding mutual sacrifice, something happens to personality which greatly enriches it. There is a participation in thought and emotion which enlarges horizons and builds new interests within. It is interesting to watch the evolution of a worker who becomes a convinced member, say, of the Socialist Party. It isn't merely that he acquires a new set of ideas or new subjects of conversation or a new language, but there is a new lift to his step, a new animation to his manner, a new authority in his voice, a new sense of his own worth. He is a different personality. Linked now with others in a cause, he is no longer merely a cog in the capitalist machine but a comrade in a human fellowship, in which he finds escape from the prison house of self and a certain measure of understanding and sympathetic response. But at best it is only a certain measure. A cause is only one great common denominator. There are many factors in each individual life not included. It is one plane on which many may meet; it does not exhaust the planes on which individual thought and feeling rove and where they crave comradeship. A Republican is always more than a Republican, a Presbyterian always more than a Presbyterian, a biologist always more than a biologist. All of them are human beings with the rich, varied, all but limitless capacities and hungers of human beings. The political or religious or scientific undertaking is only a corner of the field of their human interests and needs. Comradeship there, however complete, leaves whole areas of the self uncomraded. One man who had been closely allied with others in many struggles for a social ideal, and whom those others thought they had come to know intimately during those years of the facing of common dangers and mingling of sweat and tears, said to me: "There has never been a time, even when the battle was hottest and we were driven together for mutual re-enforcement, when I did not look at them hungrily and say to myself: 'These people do not know me. We work together and we share common perils and in so far have a mutuality of purpose, but we have never really touched the innerness of each other. They little guess the aches and longings and desolations that are here, and I suppose as little do I theirs.' " The most ardent association in a cause does not answer the poignant need we are facing now.

That is something vastly deeper, a comradeship of souls; of the innermost reality, which is not biological, which never gets into play or work; of the "you" of you, which differentiates you from every other person ever born into the world; a comradeship of "feelings that break through language and escape," of "thoughts that cannot be packed into a narrow act"; but more, of the mysterious core of selfhood on the way to personality; a comradeship which brings ultimates together so that they can think aloud without reserve and know that the other will understand or can be silent and know that the other will understand too, which makes of each self a house of many rooms and places the key to every one in the other's hand, which finds both delicately tuned instruments, each of which vibrates in sympathy when a note or a chord or a sonata is played upon the other. There are comradeships like that, not as many as there should be, but they exist, sometimes in romantic love and sometimes in a friendship like that of David and Jonathan.

II

Wherever there is this deep comradeship, there is a fulfillment of personality which cannot be rivaled by any other single experience of life. It makes possible genuine self-knowledge. One never sees himself truly except through the eyes of another who loves him. Enemies sometimes tell the truth about one. It is wisdom to listen to what they say. Their caricature gives one a slant upon himself which he needs to have. But only love can see the inwardness which explains what one is and does, an inwardness which is often hidden from one's own eyes. Nathaniel Hawthorne wrote to Sophia: "Thou only hast taught me that I have a heart—thou only hast thrown a light downward and upward into my soul. Thou only hast revealed me to myself; for without thy aid my best knowledge of myself would have been merely to know my own shadow—to watch it flickering on the wall and mistake its fantasies for my own real actions."[2] A real comrade knows us better than we know ourselves. We have lived with ourselves so long that familiarity has destroyed perspective. We have identified ourselves with a part of ourselves and have forgotten the rest; sometimes with our failures so completely that we are in despair of ourselves; sometimes with our successes so thoroughly that we have ceased to be self-critical and have become complacent. But a comrade looks at us objectively and sees both successes and failures in true proportion. From his lips, even from his eyes, we learn what our own introspections and judgments never reveal. One friend said to another, "I know you better than you know yourself." That is always true where friendship has become the intimacy which is now under consideration. Until one finds another who can enter into the deepest recesses of his soul, he himself will probably never enter but will live out his years in comparative self-ignorance.

Comradeship brings a strange but glorious enrichment. Professor Haydon, in an address before the First International Congress on Mental Hygiene, declared it "for the human multitudes perhaps the most precious value attainable and for the most highly placed intellectual the most certain guarantee of the joy of life." Professor Hocking describes it as a "power to receive and confer life at a profounder level than that of words or services." A power to receive and confer life—almost a mystical power! One cannot explain it. It waits not on time or circumstance or the communication of knowledge or training. It is as if when one soul finds another, immediately an invisible channel were established between them through which each pours his life into the other, each being enriched by all that the other is.

"Because thou hast the power and ownst the grace
To look through and behind this mask of me,

. . . .

Because thou hast the faith and love to see

. . . .

> The patient angel waiting for a place
> In the new heavens, . . .
> Teach me so
> To pour out gratitude as thou dost good."[3]

In every genuine comradeship there is a sense of "poured-out good" for which no gratitude can ever quite be the sufficient answer.

Comradeship is a great dynamic. When one finds another who means so much to him that henceforth all of life is lived to win that other's approval, when he begins to do things "for your sake," he has come upon the greatest motivating force in life. Neither logical conclusions about the quality of one's deed nor a clear vision of social results can approximate the stimulus to action which flows constantly from the desire to meet the expectations which a comrade entertains. "To be singled out as friend and comrade is often enough to remake a man."[4] If the whole story of great lives could be told—not popular lives, not successful lives, but lives which "lived above the fog in private duty and public thinking," which trod the straight, hard pathway of service to the end, which in their own sphere made bricks without straw and builded walls with the sword in one hand and the trowel in the other, which triumphed over odds and wrought nobly amid the general decay—if the story of such lives could be told, it would be discovered that the inspiration to excellence came from the knowledge that someone, whose approval meant more to them than life, was watching and would know and be proud and glad for every deed nobly wrought, every piece of work having a touch of artistry, every word fitly spoken.

Comradeship gives courage. Perivale and Lilia are talking about this very thing and Perivale says, "It means that in all your thoughts, and in all your acts, in every hope and in every fear, when you soar to the skies and when you fall to the ground, always you are holding the other person's hand."[5] "One shall chase a thousand, and two shall put ten thousand to flight." The consciousness that another is standing by, holding one's hand, understanding, does not multiply one by two but by ten. In that multiplication of courage a new fiber is imparted to personality. There is a poise, a resourcefulness, a sturdiness, a steadiness that is impressive. During one of the battles of the Civil War General Thomas Jonathan Jackson was in the line of devastating fire, exposed but undaunted. General Bee, who saw him standing there, shouted to his fellows, "Look, there is Jackson standing like a stone wall." Something of the stone wall is needed in every personality, is indispensable for its own inescapable adventures and for any effective leadership of others. A timid self will always be frightened away from those quests and conquests which alone lead to maturity of manhood. Comradeship is the great creator of courage. Once a man has found a soul who understands his purpose and believes in him whatever happens and will be there whoever else departs and will love whatever be the vicissitudes of society's admiration and contempt, he does not care very much about fate or fortune or the fickleness of society. One weighs more in his scale than the world. As long as he has one, the rest may "fold their tents like Arabs and as silently steal away" or march out with hauteur and great fuss—it does not matter. Their presence does not greatly add to his wealth; their going cannot make him poor.

> "I lean upon thee, dear, without alarm,
> And feel as safe as guarded by a charm,
> Against the stab of worldlings who, if rife,
> Are weak to injure."[6]

That is the courage which comradeship brings.

Comradeship makes one at home in the universe. Professor Bosanquet affirms that when a man is at home in the universe, he is saved. One is certainly lost in a tragic sense as long as the universe is alien to him, as long as what is within feels that there is nothing out there which is en rapport, so that one must always be on the defensive, always be misunderstood, always compelled to wage war, can never be quite at peace and at ease. But when at last one finds another who knows everything about him and likes him just the same, when longings here find an answer there, when the deepest rhythms of the soul are echoed in another, the whole situation is changed. The dominant attitude of life alters—from belligerence to benevolence, from suspicion to trust, from conflict to composure and co-operation. I remember so well watching such a change once. It took place in a man of whose brilliance of mind and integrity of purpose none ever had any doubt, but who acted like a man ringed around with enemies. His sword never slumbered in its scabbard, his sentinels were always posted, there was acerbity in his voice and acidity in his manner. He made biting speeches. He wrote vitriolic articles. He was not at home in the world. He behaved more like an army of occupation in an enemy's country. Then one day he met one who understood him, and he knew that he was understood and that a perfect understanding was compatible with perfect love. One could see him softening under the beneficent experience. The acids disappeared from his speech, the vitriol from his inkwell. He did not see any less clearly nor speak and write any less bravely, but it was the speech and writing of one who was not making war on his world but was appealing to it in the confidence that it could understand and in a measure respond. He was saved not from a theological hell but from the actual hell of an alien universe, saved to faith and trust and a sense of security, saved to a feeling of brotherhood which transformed not his words and work only but his very self.

There are other results of comradeship which might be enumerated, but they would be only variations on the essential theme and only further illustrations of what we must accept as indisputable fact. Professor Holland, of Oxford, sums it all up, "Personality lies in the relation of person to person. A personality is what it is only by virtue of power to transcend itself and to enter into the life of another. It lives by interpenetration, by communion. Its power of life is love. . . . A self-contained personality is a contradiction in terms. What we mean by personality is a capacity . . . for retaining self identity by and through identification of others—a capacity for friendship, for communion, for fellowship."[7] Cherubim, in *The Marriage of Figaro,* is more than the charming figure of Payot; he is a symbol of the universal. "The need of saying to someone 'I love you' has become so strong and imperative that I say it when I am all alone; while walking in the park I would say it . . . to you, even to the trees and to the wind."

III

The torment of life is that it so often denies people the privilege of saying that to another who responds with equal fervor and depth of meaning and consecration. The war swept under many who carried in their hearts the only answer the world provided for some.

Other hostile fates separate the living—the right persons never meet, or they meet too late, after life has been run into a mold which cannot be changed or has been set behind iron bars which only death can break. Economic disability often prevents those commitments which would link two lives in indissoluble partnership; their paths part and they go on alone. Physical handicaps sometimes lift a barrier between the heart's eternal question and its complete answer. Misunderstandings have a strange, almost devilish way of inserting themselves into promising relationships and driving apart those whom all the needs of their individual natures demand should be together in unbroken comradeship. Strange interpretations of duty lead men and women to a denial of what might be theirs could they but reach out and take it.

"No one is so accursed by fate,
No one so utterly desolate,
But some heart though unknown
Responds unto his own."

But, alas, the response often dies in thin air and the heart goes on its desolate way.

And it is a desolate way. We have spoken of the enlightening, enrichening, inspiring effects of comradeship. We could speak with equal fervor and particularity of the perverting, impoverishing, devitalizing results of that deep tragic loneliness which is not of place or of bodies, which has nothing to do with crowds or their absence but which in the depth of one's being creates a sense of desolation. There is always lamentable self-ignorance, for we only truly see ourselves in the mirror of another's loving heart; always something a bit queer, not quite normal, about anyone who cannot share his innermost; always the absence of that careless rapture of one who has someone to live for. One cannot live greatly for things, even for himself. He only dares to the limit of his powers when beloved fingers buckle on his armor as he goes out to battle, when beloved eyes watch his conduct on the field and await anxiously his safe return. There is always a struggle for faith. It is hard to believe that there is a loving, understanding heart at the center of the universe when one has not found such a heart, throbbing, incarnate in some person about him. Lloyd Morris observes that the agonized skepticism of Melville, the author of *Moby Dick,* was the result of an intolerable loneliness. More doubt than we recognize has its roots in the desolation of empty hearts. Sometimes there is rebellion against God and men. Susan Glaspel, in one of her plays, *Trifles,* tells the story of a woman whose husband was a good man according to the ethics of the countryside—he did not drink, he kept his word, he paid his debts. But he was a hard man. He gave no companionship or sympathy. When, one day, he killed the canary bird which offered her what little comradeship she had, she turned and killed him. Not often does loneliness become homicide, but shut up in the prison house of its own individuality the soul develops those rages which disturb the peace of many a group and thwart many a co-operative scheme. No one has ever tabulated the acids poured into the social stream by those who are wed but wretched in the inner life by reason of frustrated cravings for comradeship. We know how many homes are broken because marriage has not brought together two people who are able to find in each other the answer to the cry in their souls. We do not often pause to note and pity the multitude who plod bravely and charitably and sacrificially on, maintaining homes and rearing children and coming to church every Sunday, but who would give their very lives if they could escape the loneliness which oppresses them day and night and find a comrade of the deepest aspirations and anxieties and sorrows and joys of their own hearts.

One of the outstanding impressions which years of pastoral labor have made upon one man is of the multitude of lonely people there are in the world. As he arises to preach Sunday after Sunday, before a congregation gathered from elegant homes and college dormitories and modest boarding houses, there is an ache in his heart for he looks down upon wistful faces and what is even more heartbreaking, upon stolid faces which he knows are but veils drawn over the inner wistfulness.

IV

Has Jesus anything which will help the minister as he confronts this poignant human need, anything which can guide him as he seeks to guide these thwarted selves into that comradeship without which they cannot achieve fullness of personality? I do not know where we can turn with greater confidence.

He knew the significance of this quest for comradeship and gave it his blessing. Celibacy and solitude, monasticism and its mutilations will have difficulty in borrowing any authority from him. The old ritual commanded the preacher to say at every wedding, "which holy estate Christ adorned and beautified with his presence and first miracle which he wrought in Cana of Galilee." We are a bit sensitive about that miracle now, but we cannot deny that the story itself sounds very like Jesus. It never occurred to him that there was either virtue or piety in plodding a lonely way. When confronted by a question about marriage and divorce, his answer revealed an understanding of the deep yearning which prompts a man to leave father and mother and cleave to one who but a while before was an utter stranger but who stands revealed now as true comrade of the soul. His tenderness and compassion for those who loved not wisely but too well, who had blundered in their quest for comradeship, seeking in desperation that which life threatened to deny them, is strongest evidence possible of his sympathy for their need. He did not condemn them as he condemned the Pharisees who were hypnotized by wrong goals. He corrected them as one who would set right those who were on wrong trails. He impressed the men of his generation with his love of occasions which bring people together. They could not help but contrast him with the more ascetic and solitary John. So much did he frequent and encourage festive gatherings that they even called him a gluttonous man and a winebibber. He stimulated fellowship. He gathered about him an intimate company and held them together not for his sake only but also for theirs. Out of the influences he set in motion grew one of the unique things in history—a *koinonia*—a fellowship, which was the early church, which bound human hearts together in a common purpose and understanding and service, which was the astonishment of the Græco-Roman world and which eclipsed all the other guilds and fraternities then flourishing.

Not only did Jesus encourage the quest for comradeship but he clarified the formula for finding it. He emphasized love and forgiveness in every approach to each other. The significance of these virtues has not been appreciated in many of the enterprises of life and least of all in the search for companionship. Elsewhere they are important; here they are indispensable. To go through the world meeting people here and there, and, whenever you meet them, to give evidence that you are asking not "what can you give me" but "what can I give you"; not "are you so perfect that I shall never find you doing anything I need to forgive," but "forgiving always what you do, will I find in what you are the essence of that which my deepest self craves"—that is the attitude and the urgency which will discover the comrade soul among the multitude who throng the crowded ways of life. Many possible comradeships are quenched because men and women approach each other with a demand rather than a gift, with an eye for impeccable detail rather than a capacity to see the coveted fundamentals.

Jesus stressed the importance of one supreme commanding objective: "Seek ye first the kingdom of God, . . . and all these things shall be added." Among all the things which are added is this of which we are thinking now. It is forever true that in comradeship there must be a ceaseless rhythm between absorption in each other and devotion to some interest outside of themselves, which they hold in common. "I love you" must alternate with "We love books or art or music or other reality." Joy in each other, sweet and satisfying as it is, will remain sweet and satisfying only when it itself is caught up in a larger joy in something imperishable, inexhaustible. The kingdom of God is the most imperishable of all imperishables, the most inexhaustible of all inexhaustibles. All hopes and beliefs and sympathies and values which man can appreciate and God can answer are embodied in that phrase. Seekers after the blessed kingdom of another's heart must, even when they find it, gird their discovery and their further exploration with search after the kingdom of God, if the experience which unites them to another is to retain its freshness and if they are to enlarge their ministry to each other. As together they seek ever new values in the realm of God they shall find new values in each other, and thus their comradeship shall have something of infinity in it.

Jesus had another thing to say upon this subject which at first will seem to be an assault upon comradeship. "If any man come to me and hate not his father" is the vivid Oriental construction which one writer put upon his lips. "He that loveth father or mother more than me is not worthy of me" is more nearly, in the stricter phraseology of the West, what Jesus meant. The dearest comradeship must be held in a state of perpetual surrender to Christ. That is not an assault upon the sanctity and value of comradeship but its surest defense. Nothing can be prized or permanent which does not welcome the highest. We are so made that we must love the highest when we see it. Any tenure which another heart has in me or I in him, which depends upon the denial of Christ's right to both of us, is very precarious. Ultimately one of two things will happen; either Christ will win and the other be compelled to withdraw, or Christ will lose and the other will remain, but with the consciousness that that tenure has been retained by the expulsion of the best, a consciousness that will rob that tenure of its charm and ultimately render it obnoxious. Such a surrender of comradeship to Christ as will bring him into the midst of it will, on the other hand, constantly purge it of all that may mar it and invest it with a beauty that is as permanent as he is.

Significant as all these things are, and their significance can scarcely be overstressed, the real Jesus has an even greater ministry to comrade-seeking souls. He is a demonstration that the frustrations of life need not distort personality. A very learned man said to me once, "Jesus does not help us at the point of our deepest need, for our deepest need is comradeship, and Jesus never seemed to feel the strength of that need. He apparently never fell in love or wanted to. He took what fellowship the disciples offered him, blundering, sincere, but terribly inadequate, and was content with it. There is no evidence that he felt the tug of the consuming hunger for companionship of body, mind, and soul which makes going so difficult for us." That man was mistaken. There is no reason to assume that Jesus was either frigid or self-sufficient. His very tenderness toward the Magdalen and others like her is evidence that he did know that tug which leads men to find comradeship in unconventional ways when it is denied them elsewhere. His friendship with Mary of Bethany, his fondness for little children, his affection for the disciples, his compassion for the multitudes—all speak in unmistakable language of a heart that could not be content with isolation but craved understanding and fellowship and love. If he did not marry, that does not prove the absence of desire. He had a special vocation. For the sake of that vocation he denied his heart and trod a lonely road. He could not take a wife and children to Calvary with him. It was enough that his mother's heart be broken there.

Such was the unprecedented character of the task God laid upon him that even his best friends could not comprehend, and after a few months he walked the loneliest way ever entered by a loving heart. If you want final proof of his loneliness, read the story of Gethsemane. There he was, devastated by grief and praying that he might not collapse under the bludgeonings of fate. Only a stone's throw distant were his three best friends—asleep! You have never been more alone than that—a world asleep while you kept desolate vigil with unsleeping anguish; so alone that the tumult in your breast disturbed nobody.

But this man Jesus, longing for all that a comrade soul brings, losing all for the sake of his mission, nevertheless maintained perfect psychic and physical health. There is no evidence of repression; none of those functional disorders, that exaggerated curiosity, that suspicion against the purity of others, that gossipy interest in contemporary wearers of the scarlet letter which witness to submerged desire. There was none of the aversion which Paul had for all such adventures. Jesus was as wholesome as if every hunger within had found satisfaction on the highest levels, as if nature which endowed him had led him to an ideal expression of his rich endowments.

If we can capture his secret, we shall find ourselves in the possession of that which we and our world need to know, with a poignancy of need which can scarcely be exaggerated. No one ever quite recovers the secret of another's life. It is doubtful if any man ever really knows the secret of his own. There are too many influences playing upon him, too many forces stirring within him, ever to be completely observed and catalogued. But at least some of those influences and forces may be discovered. Otherwise we should be in total ignorance of ourselves and unable to help others. There are two elements in the life of Jesus which at least partly explain why he met so successfully the frustration of his desire for comradeship.

He poured himself out upon people from morn till night, upon all sorts of people, the good and the bad, the sick and the well, the ignorant and the learned, the acceptable and the outcast. He did not permit the stream of life to turn back upon itself. If others could not understand him, he would try to understand them; if they could not enter into his joys and sorrows, he would enter into theirs; if they were unable to give him that blessed experience of which Perivale spoke—"always you are holding the other person's hand"—he would at least hold out his hands to them, touch aching limb and fevered brow, pick them up when they fell, "lay a hand upon the shoulder in a friendly sort of way." That is not a perfect answer to the craving for comradeship but it does keep the craving healthy and it has its compensations in deliverance from self-pity and cynicism. And it keeps alive a sense of fellowship with one's kind.

He found in God that which men were incapable of giving him. He dared not, because of his mission, permit himself to fall in love with the loveliest woman in Galilee, but he could love God with all his heart. He could not communicate to any living person the inwardness of his life, but there was not a corner in his mind and heart that he could not unveil before his Father in heaven. He could not receive from men that understanding which he craved but he did achieve a sense that God understood. One of the most authentic sayings of Jesus is that which is recorded in Matthew. "No man knoweth the Son, but the Father: neither knoweth any man the Father, save the Son." That saying has been drafted to support a bewildering theological structure, and its real meaning has been lost from view, namely, a declaration that Jesus had such a sense of comradeship that he felt that no one in the world knew God as well as he and that no one knew him as God did. In that sense of oneness he was saved from the terrors of his human isolation and kept sane and poised and confident as he faced everything which life might bring him.

Here certainly is final wisdom for those whose craving for comradeship life has denied. We can say to the lonely folk in our congregations: "If you cannot give yourself to one, give yourself to many. Do for them what you want someone to do for you. Pour your life into a passion for understanding and helpfulness. Be comradely even when you have no ultimate human comrade. Above all, seek the fellowship of God. Jesus had it. So can you. You may not be a mystic by temperament, but somewhere along the path of moral duty, in the pursuit of beauty and truth, in public service or private prayer, you will come upon Him. Henceforth your loneliness will not be so lonely; your hunger for love will learn to say, 'O Love that wilt not let me go;' your craving to be understood will be hushed by the sense that One does understand; you will begin to dream of the time 'when the mists have rolled in splendor from the beauty of the hills,' when we shall know as we are known."

CHAPTER VIII

PERSONALITY AND MORAL FAILURE

WILLIAM WILBERFORCE, when a young man, was touring Europe. One of the books which he slipped into his luggage for reading on rainy days was Doddridge's *Rise and Progress of Religion in the Soul.* That book aroused Wilberforce from his complacency. He began to look critically at the life he had lived. It had not been a scandalous life—only selfish, a waste of time and talents. As he realized what he had been, he was seized by a sense of shame and condemnation which all the distractions of travel could not make him forget. It haunted him through hectic days and sleepless nights, until at the age of twenty-six his soul gathered itself up in one pitiful, impassioned cry—"God be merciful to me a sinner." It is a long moral leap from William Wilberforce, liberator of slaves, to Doris Mannon who, after following the gods of hate and revenge with a defiance which shouts "I ask no one to forgive me," nevertheless at the end of her mad exploits shuts herself forever within the house whose drawn blinds and uncrossed threshold are the scene of perpetual mourning. But in this tragic figure of the modern stage is the same sense of moral failure which drove the English emancipator to his knees. Both of them are a revelation of the folk who gather in our churches every Sunday and of those more numerous others who never gather anywhere except at the movie or the restaurant. Wherever two or three are gathered together, there is moral failure in the midst. And wherever men and women are in their solitudes, there also has been, or is, or will be moral failure. And that moral failure must have adequate treatment if the striving self is to achieve a healthy, social, Christian personality. Earlier I have spoken about the failure to match mental images with reality and the result of that failure in the development of paralyzing inferiority feelings, in the resort to phantasies, in the rebellions of Philistinism and the acceptances of perverted piety. But everyone who has to deal intimately with the problems of personality is aware that there is a vast difference between moral failure and all other kinds of failure and a more devastating result apparent and a more drastic remedy demanded.

I

In moral failure we are confronted with a unique experience, not definable in terms of any other, bearing in its body the marks of a truly human nature but of an aspect of human nature which is not reducible to any other element or elements in our mysterious and often awe-inspiring human heritage.

The sense of failure is not just like the consciousness of a mistake. One man sat in my presence to tell the story of an unwise decision in business which cost him a half-million dollars and left him a poor man, compelled to battle to the end of his declining strength to keep the wolf from the door. Of course there was many a sigh of regret as the tale proceeded and he thought of what might have been. Sometime later another man came. His was not a chronicle but a confession. He had stolen fifteen thousand dollars from his former associates in business. The records were all destroyed so that no trace of his defalcations remained behind to bear testimony against him. He was fifteen thousand dollars richer and they were fifteen thousand dollars poorer and none the wiser. He was safe against all prosecution but he was not safe against his own memory nor against the rebuke of his own moral ideals. He too had made a mistake, but it was more than a mistake—and when he told his story, though there were no wild sobs but only a few furtive tears, one felt the deep, dark impenetrable woe in his heart, the aftermath of an experience to which the loss of a half-million dollars was not comparable.

The sense of moral failure is not merely the consciousness of defeat. A famous surgeon, the other day, risked a delicate and dangerous operation to save the life of a much-loved minister. The effort failed and within a few hours the minister was dead, a home was broken and a church and a nation were impoverished. The surgeon was deeply grieved, for he was a great human whose patients were never merely cases. Into that operation he had put all the knowledge and all the skill acquired through a long life dedicated to the relief of pain and the defeat of death. But knowledge and skill had been in vain. Death had mocked his consecration and ridden from the field in triumph, leaving behind a much-wounded heart. But the grief evidenced in that surgeon's eyes and voice did not compare with that which his friends saw in the eyes and heard in the voice of another who had gone down to defeat, not before death but before an opportunity for easy money; who had lost not a life but a sense of his own rightness. Both were vanquished in a single experience, but the woe in the heart of one had little resemblance to that in the life of the other.

The sense of moral failure is not merely the consciousness of the violation of an external law or custom. Many times men and women have defied law and challenged custom in order to avoid a sense of moral failure. While the consciousness of moral failure often attends some breach of law or custom, frequently it does not. Even when it does, the resultant feeling is not merely one of terror at judicial penalty or fear of popular condemnation but of shame, that some principle to which one's own intelligence pays allegiance has been trampled in the dust, that some cherished ideal has been blasphemed by the reality of one's life.

Out of such surveys of human experience as have been thus briefly suggested, there emerges a conception of moral failure as a unique kind of failure—a failure to respond to perceived values, to choose the more inclusive good when one might have done so, to fulfill what the self recognized as an obligation when the ability to do so was present.

Sometimes the adverse judgment upon conduct has been fictitious because no real values were present. A professor of a great English university debated a long while with himself as to whether he ought to walk or ride the tram to his work, until one day something within him succeeded in making itself heard and said, "Don't be a fool; ride." There was no moral issue at stake and no particular failure involved, unless a failure in common sense. Methodists used to condemn themselves if in a moment of weariness they sat at cards or visited the theater. They *used* to. It would no doubt be a real moral advance if some of them could again, when they demonstrate a greater skill in contract bridge than in bidding for the soul of a city or reveal a greater familiarity with the stars of Hollywood than the Star of Bethlehem. But undoubtedly in the past some judgments upon the use of leisure time were inhuman and some feelings of moral failure were unreal.

On the other hand moral judgments are often conspicuous by their absence. "Business is business;" "A vote is a vote;" "A show is a show;" and none of them are within the range of the moral choices and moral condemnations of a lamentable number. To some it has been a matter of moral indifference whether they pay income tax. They owe nothing to the people and when the government, as representative of the people, makes demand upon them, if they can evade that demand, they are merely escaping the legal robbery. To employers in Pittsburgh and Detroit and elsewhere it is not a moral matter whether they deal with unions. They are under no obligation to organized labor or the disorganized public. They defy both and go to church on Sunday with such feelings of virtue as ought to be the monopoly of those who have wielded their power in defense of human right and divine law. To Mr. Will Hays' conscience there seems to come no sense of failure over the floods of pruriency which pass by his throne on the way from the studios to the minds of American youth. His appointment as the czar of an industry which touches the lives of seventy-seven million Americans every week and his apparent acceptance of responsibility for the guardianship of childhood have not been followed by any such apologies or penitence as the enlightened conscience of America feels ought to be forthcoming in view of the persistent assault of the screen upon those values which centuries of bitter experience have taught us are sacred and indispensable.

There is no uniformity of that moral element in men which we call conscience. Moral failure judged by objective standards often exists by the side of strange self-satisfaction. No doubt both heredity and environment enter very largely into the creation of this wide variation in occasions upon which men and women have a feeling of moral failure; heredity, perhaps, in its limitation of capacity for the appreciation of values and response to them; environment in its setting of moral patterns and in its oft imposition of a struggle so overwhelming that when one goes down he has a feeling of inevitableness. But when within whatever range of inherited capacity or within whatever pressure of environment there is a perception of values and a refusal of them, there is a sense of failure comparable with none other in its depth and intimacy. A particularly dominant image has not been matched with reality and an imperious need of the self has been frustrated.

II

The results of moral failure to personality are varied and always baneful.

Sometimes the self takes a defensive attitude against this sense of failure. The fact of it and the shame of it are thrust from consciousness and the consequences are such as always attend a repression. The person becomes a sick soul. When he would do good, evil is present with him. An inexplicable moral paralysis overtakes him. With his intellect he approves ideals, but he seems incapable of generating any enthusiasm for them. He cannot pray; petitions die in his throat. The hunger for God persists in his bosom but some subtle unbelief retards his search. He often develops functional disorders which are merely symptoms of his spiritual malady. It may be only what American youth has unanimously decided to call the "jitters"; it may be as serious as a complete nervous prostration. But whatever it be it is the warning of nature and God against a curt and peremptory dismissal of the sense of moral failure.

Often an effort is made to rationalize away the

immoral quality of this experience. Some people just cannot admit to themselves that they have been wrong. What they did was for a good purpose, and the end justified the means. The glory of God has been summoned to justify strange things—cheap, scandalous gossip, the slavery and opium trade, the crimes of capitalism, the chicanery of political machines. Or it is averred by these rationalizers that the thing just happened apart from any intention of their own and that they merely snatched what pleasure or profit they could from the episode or the situation. Or it is said that they could not help themselves. They were the victims of circumstances from which they could not escape. A mechanistic psychology has given license to a tendency which is as old as the race to achieve a feeling of innocence by placing the blame elsewhere. "The woman thou gavest me." If it wasn't a woman, it was a man or karma or fate or inherited passions or the necessities of a livelihood, or the devil—anything or anybody save the self. That age-long habit of excuse has seemed to find its charter in one school of current psychology, and under the guise of being mere biochemical organisms in reaction to environment some of our contemporaries have run amuck, trampling ideals under feet, leaving a desolate trail behind them, and have seemed to escape any compunctions about it. But whatever the scheme of rationalization employed, there are men and women who emerge from every moral failure with a sense of approval. Instead of donning stripes of condemnation they decorate themselves with medals of their own justification. They are determined not to be right but to believe themselves right. The inevitable result is a loss of moral vision. One cannot persistently refuse to perceive the actual moral nature of his deed or his own responsible part in it without dulling his perceptive capacities and ultimately forfeiting them. If there be a lost soul anywhere in God's universe, it is the man who has played fast and loose with his moral judgments, who in order to escape a sense of guilt has refused to acknowledge to himself that he is guilty and by and by has lost all power of moral appraisal; who has become morally color blind and can no longer discern between the red of danger and the green of safety, but continues to travel the roads of life, going when he ought to stop, and stopping when he ought to go, smashing and being smashed by collisions with unreckoned realities, but unable to plot a safer course. Rationalization is not less ruinous to personality than repression.

Another protective device frequently in evidence is what is familiarly known as the hardening of the heart. One can become immune against feeling. The surgeon must. If he is to perform delicate and dangerous operations with the skill which means life, he must get over the shock, the nausea, the blindness which usually accompany the first sight of a human body on the operating table and must be able to approach his patient with a degree of detachment which makes possible a clear brain and a steady nerve. The veteran goes into battle with a coolness which fills the recruit with wonder; he even jokes about his own dismemberment and expresses a jovial wish that, if he is to be draped on barbed wire, the draping may be artistically done. The judge on the bench must not permit the sway of emotions which will becloud the issue and render him less than a fair arbiter between society and its assailants. Just as nature in sheer self-defense callouses the skin which must often be chafed, so the self is capable of developing a callousness against unpleasant feelings which are the subject of constant excitation. It is a saving device and conserves energies which would otherwise be exhausted by emotional stress. But it is wrongly called into play in the moral sphere of life. Assailed by humiliation over moral failure the self, instead of seeking a remedy for the failure, hardens itself against the humiliation, develops by and by immunity against it, ceases to be morally sensitive. It is not that one does not recognize moral failure but he no longer cares.

"Who being past feeling have given themselves over," is the discerning appraisal of the New Testament.

> "Vice is a monster of so frightful mien
> As to be hated, needs but to be seen;
> Yet seen too oft, familiar with her face,
> We first endure, then pity, then embrace."

Though the most familiar of quotations, it is certainly one of the most apt delineations of the process of the gradual chloroforming of compunction. A professional man who had been fighting a losing battle against certain temptations incident to his career told me once how at the beginning he was horrified after each episode and thoroughly despised himself, but little by little the horror diminished in intensity until a deed which at first would have aroused a hurricane of feeling scarcely raised a ripple. Moral tragedies became mere social incidents, as quickly forgotten as the dropping of a handkerchief and its replacement, or the arrival of a bit of soot and its easy removal. His sin no longer hurt his feelings, but it continued to hurt him, to work its damage to his personality. He had succeeded in building up an adequate defense against regret and remorse, but in so doing had shut away the sense of reproach whose discomfort might make him cease to do evil and learn to do well. As long as there is any penitence there is hope of moral recovery, but when one who faces the moral reality of his life is past any feeling over its delinquencies, he is already beyond the pale of hope. The capacity for penitence is indispensable to the self which would achieve a robust personality. A hardening of the heart is destructive.

Sometimes the self assumes a submissive attitude to the sense of moral failure and the consequent shame. It admits the ignoble quality of the deed, and its own responsibility. There is no equivocation and no evasion and no exculpation. Before the bar of intelligence it enters a plea of guilty. It also opens the gates to all the feelings which naturally accompany such a confession—regret, remorse, disgrace.

The result is often a hypnosis. The feelings of guilt and shame are so powerful that they fasten the attention upon themselves and upon the deed which gave rise to them. And by a process which is not altogether inexplicable but which seems like a paradox, this focusing of attention results finally in a renewal of temptation and another fall. A drunkard's remorse never delivers him from his cups. It only sets the cup at the center of imagination whence appetite is aroused and ere long another spree is begun. A libertine's shame does not redeem him from his folly. It only binds him to the memory of his last experience and out of memory comes a renewal of desire which succeeds for a time in banishing shame and taking control of life. That is the deadly circle—shame, riveted attention, awakened desire, the struggle between desire and shame, the banishment of shame and the victory of desire, surrender, shame.

Submission to negative condemnatory feelings of moral failure operates in others to destroy all sense of personal worth, to beget a self-despair which cuts the nerve of all moral effort. When I preached at the penitentiary a few months ago, I told them the story of a prison dialogue. "Some men live on hope, Moike." "How much is it a package?" "It does not come in packages." "Well, it doesn't matter, it's not down on the list of things they're lettin' in here anyhow." The ripple of wistful laughter which ran through the crowd of prisoners was revelation enough that they knew what the absence of hope can do to a life. When men come to think of themselves as hopelessly in moral default with God and man and their own ideals, when the wolves of remorse eat away at their self-confidence, when self-reproach consumes self-reliance, and condemnation batters down all aspiration, whether men be in prison or out, there ensues an abandonment of the struggle. "Oh, well, what's the use? It isn't in me. I was not born to be a saint;" and with that valedictory they turn their back upon high purpose and heroic commitment and descend into the slums of life.

Even where there remains an allegiance to ideals and an effort for their attainment there is only a sorrowful tale to be told as long as the heart is the abode of guilt and shame. The negative feelings are not only a source of crippling misery, the destruction of all peace, the foe of all clear thinking, but they are like a ball and chain upon the feet of resolution. They may become a disease. The classic illustration is the author of *The Pilgrim's Progress*. After a rather wild youth he reformed and developed a conscience so sensitive that he dare not take a pin or a stick though but so big as a straw. But all the while his former sins haunted him. Wanting to get rid of his sense of guilt, he was nevertheless afraid that he might lose it without actually receiving remission for his sins. "For two years nothing could occupy his mind but damnation and the expectation of damnation." "It was only because Bunyan succeeded in emerging from his unhealthy condition of mental pain and marked preoccupation about his own damnation," that we have ever heard of him or his obsessions.[1] Of most cases in our own time we do not hear until they finally arrive at some mental clinic. How numerous they are we do not know. There is a moral flippancy in the air which persuades some observers that nobody worries about his sins any more. The common conclusion is that the only thing which disturbs the average American is ignorance of the dictums of Emily Post or a slump in the market. The use of a wrong fork at the dinner seems to many more lamentable than a wrong approach to a great social problem; a drop in A. T. & T., more ominous than the fall which reveals that the flesh still dominates the spirit. But underneath all the absorption in manners and money is still a sense of right and wrong and, as one discovers who lives intimately with people, a great deal of misery because that sense of right and wrong has been violated and the violators do not know what to do about it.

III

Three great needs of the self on the way to personality emerge from this survey of moral failure. First is a thoroughgoing realism, which will recognize failure as failure, will not be scared but sobered by it, will not rationalize it away but be reasonable about it, will not project it upon others but will keep it at home where it belongs, will not harden the heart against the normal feelings which failure brings but let them make their own appeal. There is no competent treatise anywhere that does not assume as the basis of all spiritual help what Stekel calls "a reconciliation with reality," and what Miss Coster describes as "the objective facing of real facts in regard to oneself and one's environment" and the "deep, humble, open-armed acceptance of them." Only a self which makes such reconciliation with reality not merely an occasional honesty but its habitual attitude can deal wisely with its moral failures.

Second, the achievement of a sense of forgiveness; that one's sin is no longer held against him; that whatever happened yesterday to-day is a new day brooded over by hope and love; that one labors to-day not under the lash of divine reproach but under the caresses of divine encouragement; that God is not a spiteful supervisor who never forgets but a generous Father who is more anxious to obliterate all remembrance of failure than we are; that he is never so disgusted with the number of times the fires of moral resolution have flickered and gone out, that he abandons us but, rather, is so happy over every spark of moral purpose which remains that his whole attention is consumed in an effort to fan it into a flame. The sense of forgiveness must not make sin cheap, as if it were merely a false comma in a story written on the slate of life, easily rubbed out and forgotten. That kind of forgiveness does not encourage resolution. It promotes laxity. Redemptive forgiveness must be free and full, but it must be forgiveness which reveals that it comes, not from a heart to which sin has made no difference but from a heart which can match every sin, no matter how great, with a greater love. Only thus can the dark reality of yesterday be seen to be the dark reality it was and yet thrust aside by the promise of to-day and to-morrow.

Third, an escape from the bondage of the hypnosis or the habit of moral failure; the achievement of an actual freedom. Religion has sometimes failed to recognize how much we are bound by our past, how all ideas and emotions which we have ever had form what Taine calls "a singularly solid network," and that it does require "a great accumulation of forces to tear from it any portion really belonging to it." The solidity of this network is guarantee of the integrity of the self and is its citadel against disintegration. But it is also a problem when in that network are ideas and emotions connected with moral failure. Only a force strong enough to change the very warp and woof of the self is competent to affect deliverance from unworthy patterns which have been woven on the loom of the past, and set one free for the realization of nobler patterns.

IV

Has Jesus anything to offer which will help the growing self meet the needs arising out of its own moral failures? Our fathers used to proclaim him as Saviour from the guilt of sin and the power of sin. Is he, or did the help which they apparently received from him actually come from a theological phantasy? Professor Pratt, in summarizing the experience of John Bunyan, wrote, "Poor Bunyan eventually got out of his trouble in the same way he got into it, that is to say, by the obsession of Scripture verses. . . . Bunyan's real conversion was the inner change of values that took place somewhere between his self-centered youth and his truly Christian years in Bedford jail. . . . The conversion which he has described to us and which has been held up as a splendid example by all the generations of evangelical teachers from his day to ours is almost entirely a matter of feeling and has little more moral significance than the struggle which most of us have experienced between two haunting and obsessing tunes which go running on in a man's mind till one drives the other out."[2] Was the fascination which Jesus had for other generations merely "the obsession of Scripture verses" and theological ideas? Were the real conversions which took place the result of influences which originated in other sources than Jesus and the supposed conversions merely the conquest of one tune by another? And is it true now, since we can no longer yield to the obsession of Scripture verses and the ideas of antiquated theology, nor be deluded by a mere transposition of tunes, that we must look elsewhere than to Jesus for an adequate treatment of moral failure such as will help us truly to become persons? The answer is an unhesitating "No." The theological Jesus of yesterday may not answer our needs. The repetition of random Scripture verses may have lost their power. But the Jesus of history is still the Saviour of those who will live in spiritual fellowship with him. Schweitzer's memorable word stands, independent of his or any other critical theories about Jesus.[3]

Consider for a moment the teaching of Jesus. We have said that the first need of the self is a thoroughgoing realism. Was there ever a teacher who more earnestly pleads for that? Recall his parable of the rationalizers who tried to explain away or justify their refusal of obligation. "And they all with one consent began to make excuse. The first said unto him, I have bought a piece of ground, and I must needs go and see it: I pray thee have me excused. And another said, I have bought five yoke of oxen, and I go to prove them: I pray thee have me excused. And another said, I have married a wife and therefore I cannot come." Each was a plausible excuse, but plausible only to the maker of it. Some Americans bought some land in Florida without seeing it, land which they later discovered was not land but water, a place for boats instead of houses. But that is a modern method of purchasing real estate. They knew nothing of it in Palestine. The man had seen the land, and it would be there next week. The yoke of oxen could be tried just as well later. The married man might have taken his wife along, or if she were not invited he could have left her at home. Such things have been done in peace and in war when social obligation or civic duty demanded. No one can read that parable and not be spurred to a re-examination of his own refusals of the call of duty. Remember Jesus' brilliant characterization of two men who went up into the temple to pray, one a Pharisee and the other a publican. The man who faced the real facts about himself, who did not harden himself against the feeling of shame but smote his breast in the reality of his penitence, this man went down to his house justified rather than the other. How Jesus scorned the hypocrite who set a false image of himself not before the eyes of others only but also before his own eyes! How he pleaded that men would come up to the light, that their deeds might be reproved! How he reminded them that their Father seeth in secret, that there is nothing hidden that shall not be revealed, that what is whispered in the ear shall be shouted from the housetops! How he pitied the man who could see a splinter in the eye of another but was unaware of the plank in his own! If there is any one element in the teaching of the historical Jesus that is beyond question, it is its constant, consistent plea for what our psychologists call a thoroughgoing realism.

That plea for realism was utterly free from any suggestion of morbidity. He encouraged repentance but not remorse. "How many weak souls were driven to despair or madness or vice by threats of hellfire and thunders against the filthiness of human righteousness we do not know."[4] But we do know that they were never driven there by Jesus; only by preachers who never saw the real Jesus. One hymn may compel us to sing, "For such a worm as I," but Jesus never asked us to sing anything like that. Another may say in penitent emotion, "And let me weep my life away for having grieved thy love," but Jesus, the great Lover himself, never hinted that that was a profitable way to spend the rest of one's life. Coming to men with more searching ethical demands than they had ever known, urging them to recognize their failures to rise to those demands and to accept responsibility for those failures, nevertheless he sought constantly to turn their eyes to the future instead of the past, to live not in an orgy of self-accusation, nor in a cloud of fear in divine wrath but in the assurance of God's Fatherly and gracious forgiveness. The significance of that emphasis upon forgiveness can be understood only by a return to that history in the midst of which we are trying to recover Jesus' reality. The world to which he came was a world dominated either by Jewish or Hellenistic ideas. But in neither Judaism nor Hellenism was there any reconciliation of the ideas of justice and mercy. As Goguel has so thoroughly indicated,[5] in Judaism there was a ritual expiation for sin; there was an unexplained clemency toward a chosen people; there was a notion that good works could compensate in a measure for sin. But wherever in Jewish thought the ideas of divine justice and holiness have been fully maintained, there was no room for the idea of pardon. Neither could Hellenism admit the idea of forgiveness. Plato declared that "the most impious of all the impious are those who think the gods could betray the strict justice of which they are guardians." Celsus ridiculed the Christian God as the captain of a robber band who gathers a company of evildoers around himself. In Hellenism purification always had to precede contact with God. It was into a world dominated by such ideas that Jesus came, proclaiming the free and limitless forgiveness of God. In parable after parable, in his own contacts with sinners, he revealed a conviction which was fundamental, that the way to meet moral failure is to hide it neither from oneself nor from God and to brood over it not at all, but to bring it to God who will always meet penitence with a forgiveness which, as far as God and ourselves are concerned, leaves the situation as if no sin had ever been, save that in the heart of the forgiven man there is a new gratitude and a new love which are born out of God's grace in forgiveness and which become a new and powerful incentive to righteousness. I talked with a father whose boy had given him a lot of trouble. One failure after another had frustrated the father's plans and mocked his dreams, but the lad was still trying, and his letters revealed a determination yet to make good and make a life. As the father talked to me, I knew that the past was not on the record against the boy, that the only thing the father was interested in was the future, and that the only thing that the years had done to the father had been to intensify his interest and quicken his devotion and surround it all with a beautiful tenderness which the boy's many failures and repentances and continued struggles had called into being. When those letters were related to me, I knew that the boy, instead of brooding over failures deep and dark enough to discourage anybody and being bound by that brooding to a miserable history, had by his father's forgiving love been redeemed from the spell of yesterday and been enabled to look ahead to possibilities of triumph and inspired to continue the struggle of making possibilities actual achievements. And whenever I think of that father and that boy, I think that is how Jesus wanted us to think of God and of ourselves and our failures—as a challenge to try again, energized by a consciousness that God believes in us and broods over us and stands by to help.

V

The unique ministry of Jesus to this aspect of human need is not merely in what he taught. It is in what he did to make that teaching convincing.

He lived a superlative life. Such generous ideas of forgiveness would not be very impressive if uttered by some lips. Men are apt to condone that of which they themselves are guilty. Loose lives are often very liberal in their moral judgments, but their judgments are by their own practice put under question. A man struggling with a sense of wrong finally went to another and confessed. He received for his confession a ready absolution and went away comforted. It helped him to recover his self-respect and his peace of mind. If that other person could forgive, no doubt God would too. It was like a double pardon, one from earth and one from heaven. Then one day he learned that that other person had been guilty of the same moral failure. Instantly his own peace and assurance of forgiveness departed. If that other person were guilty of the same sin, perhaps his ready forgiveness was the result of a clouded judgment or of a wish that his own dereliction might be as generously handled. Maybe it was a case of being merciful in order to obtain mercy. If that other had been innocent, perhaps he would not have been so ready to absolve guilt. At any rate *his* reaction was no assurance of God's reaction. The old tumult returned. The forgiveness of sinners by sinners is a wholesome, human experience, but not necessarily an echo of the divine experience.

Jesus does not enter that category. Without beginning any foolish and useless debate about the sinlessness of any historic character, we can all agree that Jesus is the superlative character of history. An unimpeachable moral judgment was accompanied by an unimpeachable life. Here is the most Godlike person the world has ever granted a brief domicile. When the most Godlike in the realm of our acquaintance forgives, it is like hearing God forgive. When he assures that God does forgive, we are assured. His character gives us confidence in his insight. His life makes him a competent witness to the Life that is beyond life.

The forgiveness Jesus offered men in behalf of

God was a convincing forgiveness. Men cannot be helped by an easy forgiveness. It is not adequate to the deep and tragic sense of need which comes to a morally awakened soul. Many of you have read T. C. Wren's story, *The Coward of the Legion*. The hero is Jean Dubonnet, who received a medal for gallantry in action but who later, when a comrade was congratulating him, broke loose in a volley of self condemnation, declaring himself an abject coward. The mystery was explained when Dubonnet confessed that he had loved a woman whom he could not marry and who with him decided that if they could not live together, they would die together. The woman took the poison but Jean weakened. She died and he lived. His friends despised him and branded his name upon his breast with the words "Liar" and "Coward." It was the irony of that *croix de guerre* on his coat and that brand underneath which filled him with self reproach. Nor did he find redemption until that brand had been burned out as it had been burned in. In the agonizing pain of the burning he found release from the cowardice of yesterday and became a man again and died as a brave soldier. To those who have not looked squarely at their own moral failure, nor lived intimately with the failure of others, that tale seems almost grotesque. But some of us know how real was the demand in that soldier's breast for an expiation. To say to him, "Forget it; you proved your courage by winning that *croix de guerre*," was only to tantalize him. He could not forget unless somewhere the memory had been answered by suffering. I had to deal with a man who had committed an assault upon his own cherished ideals. His grief and remorse were terrible. They played havoc with his life. He was a student, but books no longer charmed him. He was a lover of nature, but the bluest sky hovered over him like a harbinger of doom. He had won honors, but honors were as hateful to him as that soldier's *croix de guerre*. He tried to pray, but his sense of his own demerit rose like a cloud of mustard gas between him and God, choking every utterance. He had been an advanced theological liberal, and from his thinking had long since departed any acceptance of the old doctrine of the atonement. It seemed to his logical mind absurd to assume that the death of a good Man upon a cross of shame could in any sense atone for the sins of anyone else, let alone the sins of the world; or to believe that a loving God could ask for such a painful but futile gesture. But during those days when he was confronted by the dark disaster of his own sin, and was groping his way back to life again, the only thing which brought him any relief was the remembrance of the suffering love of Jesus. In a way which he could not explain to himself, when he thought of that Man suffering there and loving the sinners who inflicted the suffering and taking into his own heart the shame of their sins he found courage to pray and to hope for the forgiveness of God. Calvary spoke to his heart the word of peace.

There is something very real here. I have never read a doctrine of the atonement that gave me any satisfaction. All seem to me either to ignore the reality of history, that is, how Jesus actually came to die, or to impeach the character of God. But in the relation of the sufferings of Jesus to the word of forgiveness is a clue to a satisfying explanation of the significance of the cross for moral failure. At least it is to one man who is trying to be real in his own moral life and helpful to others in their struggles. I like what Mackintosh, of Edinburgh, has to say here, "When by self-conquest which even bystanders can see to be noble, the injured man, refusing to ignore moral realities, yet reaching over and beyond the wrong to knit up old ties of communion, attains to the act of deep pure pardon, the act presupposes and is mediated by costly suffering."[6] Forgiveness does involve suffering. The question in the serious heart when it sins against man or God is always this: "Will the one I have wronged endure the suffering necessary to forgive me completely?" That is where doubt arises and there only in an affirmative answer can faith be born and a sense of forgiveness achieved. There has never been such an affirmative answer given as at the cross. There hung One who endured the greatest wrong; the best was maltreated by the worst; the noblest was made the victim of the most terrible physical torture, awful moral contempt, ultimate social degradation, crucified as the enemy of God and man, fit only to be spit upon and to die. But he forgave. He demonstrated that there is in the universe a spirit which can "reach over and beyond the worst wrong and seeking to knit up the old ties of communion, attain to an act of deep, pure pardon." Hanging there he prayed, "Father, forgive them." One can believe that that prayer is answered and will be answered always in such a presence. The forgiveness of Jesus was a convincing forgiveness. It paid a price. And when he talks about the forgiveness of God, we know that it is not the glib utterance of one who is too superficial to realize what forgiveness involves, but one who realizing it as none other ever has, nevertheless is confident that God will, as he did, forgive every returning prodigal. Listening to him we can take up the old litany.

"My God is reconciled,
His pardoning voice I hear,
He owns me for his child,
I can no longer fear."

Finally Jesus actually becomes a deliverer from moral failure. That deliverance arises first as the result of the forgiveness which he makes so real. The memory of sin no longer remains to act as a hypnotic influence leading to repetition. The mind and heart are free to become occupied with other and worthier themes and projects. And in forgiveness gratitude and love are born, which in turn become a powerful stimulus to please the One who has been so gracious. Helen Waddell has described with a faithfulness which escapes the writing of cold history, what happened to Abelard, self-condemned, and yet resisting the insufferable patronage of the saints. Into his heart there floated the forgiving word of Jesus, "Neither do I condemn thee. Go and sin no more." "His rage dropped from him. . . . He sat down . . . and dropped his head on his hands. 'And because He would not condemn me I could lay my head in the dust.' "[7] Later another struggle comes upon him. "Grief without a ripple, without ebb or flow, a kind of dark water lay sullen in his heart. And he was again in rebellion. And again came the frail wisp of memory, voiceless as the drift of thistledown, inevitable as the sunrise, 'Neither do I condemn thee.' For a moment it seemed to him that all the vital forces of the body were withdrawing themselves. . . . Then his spirit leaped toward heaven in naked adoration; . . . with every power of his mind, with every pulse of his body he worshiped God."[8] It was forgiveness that had brought deliverance. Where exhortation and denunciation alike had failed, the sense of God's mercy freed him from his past and set in his heart a passion for goodness and God.

If men and women are ever to achieve Christian personality, we must help them with their moral failures. And I know no better formula for our preaching than that we should let them see the real Jesus of whom these feeble words have been an inadequate picture.

CHAPTER IX

THE REALIZATION OF JESUS

WE have come to the end of a hurried journey through the ever-fascinating, ever-baffling continent of personality. We have made no pretense at anything like a complete tour. We have merely looked at a few strategic and embattled points where the fiercest struggles have been waged and the greatest defeats suffered and the noblest victories won. We have tried to make clear how strategic those points are; that if the ever-striving self can discover how to deal wisely with appealing mental images, how to achieve an abiding self-respect, how to satisfy the deep, pervasive need for comradeship, how to solve the problem presented by moral failure, there is a foundation laid for those further conquests which must be made ere the self achieves fullness of personality. We have found the historical Jesus an ever-present source of wisdom and an unfailing inspiration in the approach to each of these places of difficulty. It has been our hope that these brief and inadequate explorations may remind the ministry once again of some perennial struggles which confront and baffle the souls whom they are called to shepherd, struggles which either mar personality or mold it into beauty and power. It has been hoped too that this partial analysis of specific needs of the striving self and the revelation of their answer in Jesus will inspire further analysis and revelation on the part of those whose supreme responsibility is personality.

In this closing chapter I address myself to my fellow-preachers particularly. Much of our preaching is ineffective because we do not know what the struggles of our people are. What we say to them on Sunday is as inapplicable to their urgent needs as a lecture on cosmic rays would be to a man suffering with the colic. There are places where lectures on cosmic rays are in order, but certainly not in a clinic for disordered stomachs. There probably have been few themes discussed in the American pulpit which do not have their appropriate forum, but that forum is not in the presence of an audience of people who have a right to expect counsel in their difficult strivings to become persons. Only a genuine interest in the people who attend our ministry and a vivid understanding of their needs artificial and real, and of the conflicts into which those needs precipitate them, and of the deforming, mutilating, paralyzing effects of those conflicts, and of the spiritual therapy which can eliminate those effects, and of the personal strategy which can give the real and fundamental needs some satisfying answer—only this can make our preaching a real ministry to personality—a creation and re-creation of souls.

At the beginning of the series I expressed my profound appreciation of those who are preaching for a more Christian social order which shall give striving selves a real chance to become persons. I declared not merely my hope that the church would give them a charter to continue but my purpose to remain in alliance with them as far as I am able to share their vision both of goals and of methods, and to permit them to make no personal sacrifice in behalf of the establishment of the kingdom of God on earth which I myself do not match as far as God shall give me grace. I should regret beyond all power of language to express, if anything said in these lectures should be used to raise again that false antithesis between the simple gospel and the social gospel, or be made a pretext for casting even a pebble at the brave men in our pulpits who are bringing just and damning indictments against the iniquities and inequities and moral degradations of a social order dominated by the profit motive and characterized by a sickening alternation between the frenzies of so-called prosperity and the furies of a real depression; who are seeking an end of the irrational paradox of blighting poverty in a world which has ample material resources for all; who are taking desperate risks to break the hypnotic spell of armaments and the inevitable catastrophes to which such a hypnotism leads. I would not diminish the number of these prophets nor soften one syllable of their often harsh speech. A soft answer may turn away wrath, but soft words will not overturn the organized evils of our day nor destroy a system which appeals to the predatory tendencies in human nature and gives them almost unlimited license. This author does not feel worthy to unloose the sandals of many of these crusaders for a better world, and he certainly will have no part nor lot with those who would unfrock them nor quench the fire in their hearts.

What he has been trying to say is that so often in our absorption in the reformation of systems we have forgotten man. We have not balanced our indictment of social evil with our diagnosis of the ailments of persons. We have not matched our social remedies with effective prescriptions for those individual ills which afflict our people. In attempting to hasten the coming of the kingdom of God on earth we have not always remembered that there is a kingdom to be established in individual hearts. In telling men how to vote, or how to settle industrial disputes, or how to run governments, we have often failed to tell them how to elect ideals or reconcile conflicting impulses or to bring everything into captivity and obedience to Christ. These ought we to have done and not to have left the other undone. We shall not have ideal personalities in any number until we have an ideal society. But neither shall we have an ideal society until we have ideal personalities. In the meantime there is much that we can do to help people understand themselves, untangle the twisted skein of self, satisfy deep and urgent needs, direct the misdirected energies, find poise and power, if we ourselves study more earnestly to know what is in men and reconstruct our preaching in the light of that knowledge. Physicians ought to have an interest in social sanitation. The hope of a healthy human race depends upon the abolition of germ-breeding slums and infected food and water supplies, upon adequate sewage disposal, and the isolation of contagious diseases and the disinfection of homes and public buildings and trains. But if physicians devoted themselves exclusively to agitation in behalf of these important reforms, the race would have a rather sorry time of it. I was glad a week ago that some men in my city thought it worth while to be interested in broken arms and to know what to do with them when they made a midnight call; were prepared to take X-ray pictures and probe the flesh for shattered bits of bone and reset dislocated joints and restitch severed muscles. The noblest appeal ever made for proper sidewalks and traffic guards and other defenses for the unwary would have been only an irritation to the urgent personal need that was mine. More than some of us have guessed we have been expending eloquent social appeals upon people with some brokenness of life which demanded attention. They have come and gone from our ministry, unhealed, afflicted with unguessed pains and miseries, ultimately crippled almost beyond the hope of cure, because we have despised or neglected the healing of souls in our absorption in what we have called the larger task. It is to lift a small voice in behalf of individuals whose pains and perplexities cannot await the arrival of Utopia but must have immediate help that I write. This I do with a conviction that in so doing there is no impeachment of the religion of social passion but, rather, a discussion of those personal factors without whose adequate treatment the religion of the social passion will never find its fulfillment.

I

Our thesis has been that the Jesus of history in a unique and indispensable fashion offers counsel and inspiration to all struggling selves on their way to personality. It was said of him by a preacher of long ago, "There is none other name given under heaven or among men whereby we must be saved." That affirmation, like many others found in the New Testament, has been made the authority for all sorts of intolerable theologies, for the religious disfranchisement of noble spirits in other religions, for the consignment to eternal torment of millions who in loyalty to their ancestors, or as the result of the training of childhood, sought God by some other way. But behind that sweeping statement is an important aspect of reality. Studying the striving self with as impartial eyes as science can provide us, it is difficult to discover how that self may come at last to completeness of personality except along lines indicated by Jesus in his teaching and life. If the name of Jesus be taken to mean not a mere talisman whereby the gates of heaven may be opened but the symbol of all that Jesus said and did, his character and counsel, then it is not theology but life which declares that there is none other whereby the self can achieve its fullest possibilities in a balanced, sturdy, moral personality. That has been the thesis of this series. In so brief a time we could not prove, we could only illustrate our meanings, point to some answers which have been given, and indulge in the hope that these answers will inspire further explorations for the sake of that flock which every preacher is called to feed and to whose nurture preaching ought to be a major contribution.

II

In this concluding chapter I want to ask what all that we have been saying involves for the pulpit, and how preaching may more effectively help men and women to appropriate the values that are in Jesus for the liberation, unification, and enrichment of their own personalities. There are two prevalent tendencies in the modern pulpit which greatly weaken the effectiveness of its ministry to personality.

One is the blurring and sometimes practical exclusion of Jesus, the presentation of current topics, abstract philosophies, hypotheses of science, witticisms, epigrams, histrionics, the preacher himself, everything except Jesus. A man might attend some ministries a long time and not learn very much about Jesus, the substance of his teachings, or the quality of his life. He is referred to. He is even quoted. But little is done to present him in such fashion that he can be taken either as example or guide, even by those who are searching for one. As for the revelation of his charm there is none. There used to be in circulation the story of a brilliant young preacher who went to his first church full of pride in his diligently acquired learning and in his ability to put that learning on forensic display. His congregation had a certain pride too in this newly acquired product of the theological seminary, with two degrees after his name and many ohs! and ahs! after his breathless perorations. But they missed something. One day, when the young man entered his pulpit, crammed with reason and rhetoric, he saw a note pinned on his pulpit sofa, bearing the legend, "Sir, we would see Jesus." The story had it that the fire died out on the altar of learning that day, and ere he returned to the pulpit again he had builded another altar, and above it was a form like unto the Son of man, and they who came to be thrilled remained to pray. On a later Sunday the young minister found another note pinned on the pulpit sofa which read, "Then were the disciples glad when they saw the Lord." There was a time in my ministry when that story irritated me. It seemed to me to be a slur upon education and an assumption that the minister's task demanded less brain sweat and more fluency as a teller of gospel stories. It seemed to be a plea in exemption from hard thinking on the part of the laymen and an apotheosis of unintelligent pietism. But the longer I live and wrestle with the art of preaching, the more timeless that story seems to be. There are many congregations where that plea would be in place. "Sir, we would see Jesus."

They see everything else but him. That is the first great threat to an effective ministry.

The second is like unto it. Jesus is much praised by name but never revealed in his thrilling, vitalizing reality. A very discerning listener who is on the quest for the highest spiritual values sat by my side on a sacred day, listening to a number of addresses by leading ministers. Those addresses were all about Jesus. I was curious to know what impression had been made upon my friend and at the first opportunity began a conversation about what we had heard. I asked him no leading question. I wanted to get his personal reaction, his dominant impression. Almost immediately he said: "It is strange to me how much some ministers can talk about Jesus and not really tell anything about him. They keep saying over and over again that he is Lord and Saviour without giving you any clue as to what constitutes his Lordship or in what sense and how he actually does function as a Saviour. I came away having heard a lot of words but little that would bring Jesus into a morally and spiritually creative relation to my life." Abstraction, generalization, verbalization, are the besetting sins of the ministry. People are urged to "come to Jesus," to "accept Jesus as Saviour," to "believe on Jesus," to "profess Jesus," but are not given any specific directions which will make those exhortations something more than mere evangelistic verbiage or provide for those who hear them a technique for the appropriation of those rich values for personality which are found in him. The result is that many who sing most easily "Jesus saves" are not saved from the ills which mar life. They believe with much assurance but are not blessed with any noticeable deliverance from crippling tendencies in human nature. They accept Christ but are not any more acceptable than some who are said to reject him. They "come to Jesus" but do not seem to be as near to his moral and spiritual beauty as many who apparently stay away.

My closing plea is for such preaching as will bring to people all the values for personality that are found in Jesus and that will teach them how to lay hold on those values in the Ideal Person for the enrichment of their own persons. Something of the passion of Saint Paul, "My little children for whom I do travail in birth again until Christ be formed in you," must enter into the preaching of every age if that preaching is to become a significant force in the making of the new humanity. Until Christ be formed in you! Not merely given pulpit recognition, not simply talked about, but formed in you, yourself becoming such a person that people who know you will be compelled to think of the Ideal Person, will see something of his splendor and abundance and unity and vigor and poise in you. That is the purpose of preaching, a purpose whose fulfillment makes peremptory demands upon us.

III

First, that we shall let people have through our preaching the redemptive influence of the ideas of Jesus. On an earlier page we affirmed our confidence in the value of ideas for the striving self, and all that we said there applies with special potency to the ideas of Jesus. We lose from our ministry forces of incalculable influence when we exclude or just forget the thought-world of the Man of Galilee. Some things which are said about expository preaching do not greatly impress me. It certainly has little authority from the greatest of all preachers. He did not proceed, as far as we are able to determine, either by quotation or exegesis. He came to a people who were saturated with expositions of ancient authorities and he came with a fresh approach to reality and to specific life problems. He knew what the fathers had said but he felt compelled to say something different. "Ye have heard it said—but I say." He knew the law and he reverenced it, but he knew people too, and he reverenced them more. Their burdens and sorrows and struggles and sins stung him to the quick and became the theme of his preaching. He seemed always to be speaking directly to people about matters which vexed and vanquished them. He did not take a passage from the law or the prophets, unravel its general principles, and then look about to discover if there were some place where those principles might be having an immediate application. Rather did he address himself to the human situation before him, guided by familiarity with the moral vision of yesterday but also by his own fresh and unique insight. He was, if anything, a topical preacher, talking about themes of immediate interest to the people before him. He had what we moderns call the problem approach. His homilies were suggested by incidents of the day, incidents which he always lifted into the light of eternity, but still incidents of the day, not the indictments of some far yesterday. After following his ministry in an effort to learn something about our own, there is no longer any peculiar sanctity for some of us in expository preaching as a method. But we are convinced that whatever the type of sermon used, it will always be nonproductive if through it there do not stream the illuminating, arresting ideas which characterize Jesus' outlook upon life; and it will inevitably, in spite of all the failures of the preacher in logic and rhetoric, be a sermon which will help some struggling soul if some of those creative ideas succeed in breaking through the fog of the preacher's mind and the fumble of his speech. Those ideas have a unique appeal. There is something in them congenial to the human mind. While they affront many of its vanities and deny many of its impulses, so that there is peculiar aptness in the word of Saint Paul, "The natural man understandeth not the things of God," nevertheless they reach in behind the clamors of appetite and the assertions of pride and get hold of a man. He may try to forget but cannot. He must have dealings with them. A history of ideas would reveal what capacity the ideas of Jesus have of domiciling themselves in the mind of man and influencing character and determining conduct. If they only have a chance! Our first responsibility is to give them a chance, to let them be heard from our lips, to permit them to inspire and inform our preaching. It ought to be impossible for men and women to attend our ministry for a year or two without becoming rather thoroughly acquainted, not merely with the dominant ideas in our minds but with the master ideas in the mind of Jesus. Sermon series in which the major emphases of Jesus are linked together in a living whole have great value. Laymen confess their ignorance of what Jesus really believed on matters of great importance to them, and after every such series come to express gratitude as they say in one fashion or another, "I never before understood the mind of Jesus about this question." But of greater value is it for the preacher to have his own mind so saturated with the ideas of Jesus that he cannot help letting those ideas shine through every public utterance until his hearers become illuminated by their searching light. One minister relates with peculiar joy a testimony to his preaching uttered by one who brought to church a discriminating intelligence, "We have never had a preacher who gave us so much of Jesus." He was not a conventional preacher. He took all sorts of pulpit themes. He was especially interested in the scientific approach to religion. He was quite unorthodox. Those who doted on familiar phrases went away disappointed. But through all his variation from conventional preaching there played such a constant influence from the mind of Jesus that whatever else had happened, those who listened seriously had gained a clearer understanding of that royal mind than had come through the more conventional homiletics of his predecessors. That was an achievement. The values of Jesus for personality are, first of all, the values inherent in his idea of life, and our first great concern should be to release those ideas upon the minds of this generation. That in itself is a task demanding our greatest capacity for interpretation. It involves disentangling the ideas of Jesus from the ideas of his friends and reporters—a labor which a previous generation, beguiled by false notions of inspiration, repudiated as unnecessary but which historical realism knows now to be imperative if we are to proclaim the real Jesus rather than some lesser mind's unwitting distortion of him. It involves often a disentangling of the ideas of Jesus from his own words. Because of traditional interpretations which have surrounded them, or even because of a change in forms of speech, the mere repetition of his words awakens in the minds of our congregations ideas which are utterly foreign to the mind of Jesus. A recital of words is not always the revelation of ideas. Often the largest service anyone can render his generation is to capture an old idea and clothe it in current speech. The men who are doing most to release the mind of Jesus upon the minds of our contemporaries are men who are subsidizing current idioms in behalf of Christian ideas. With some men it seems to be a gift. They have an almost uncanny ability to restate the ideas of the Master in language which not only arrests attention but actually communicates the truth, and they are the envy of all the rest of us. But we can and must toil arduously in the effort to make vivid and real to the struggling souls before us the wisdom of Jesus.

Second, that wisdom must be creatively imparted. It must become not a dogma but an inspiration; not an embargo upon thinking but a stimulus to unhampered mental activity. Some preachers make prison walls out of the reported ideas of Jesus and attempt to confine people to the area thus inclosed—an impossible limitation for sturdy, honest realists to accept. Jesus did not have ideas about some subjects concerning which we must have ideas if we are to live. Some ideas which he had would no doubt be modified in the presence of situations which did not confront him but do confront us. The slavish imitation of his ideas is a dishonor to him and a disability which will seriously hamper the self which is trying to become a person in the modern world. His ideas should be presented not as mere patterns to follow but as inspiration to men to make their own thought patterns in the light of their own immediate personal problems. One of the most suggestive things which has been written upon this subject appears in a recent book, *I Follow the Road,*[1] a book written by a society leader whose path is far removed from that trodden by the saints, who lives in a world of social brilliance, who is apparently at home with the latest in music and art and literature, who was once more at ease with cigarettes than with the cross and was disdainful of parsons and religion generally. She exposed herself to the ideas of Jesus and was called out to an adventure for which probably no preacher could have been the pilot but which finally led her over strange routes, through nights without stars and days without sun, to the place where she affirms, "It isn't likely that I can be mistaken for a saintly person in these pages or in life. . . . But I am at least a person to whom Christ is a joy, whose activities join ever so faintly the hope of beauty that is the quest of gifted youth." In the brief sketch of her adventure this woman discloses a practice which she not only employed effectively but recommended helpfully to others, the practice of making mental patterns with a mind toned up by the reading of the New Testament. "After reading of the nobility of Christ your mind will function on a new and higher level," she wrote to a friend in trouble. To another she said, "I do practice lifting my life to the level of thoughts that come to me after reading the New Testament." Strange, isn't it, that one so far from the beaten path of religion should stumble upon so sublime a secret, the use of the teachings of Jesus not to furlough the mind by giving it ready-made formulas, but to quicken it to find the right solution of its conflicts and a satisfying adjustment to the frustrations which life perpetually brings? I wonder if we preachers have so preached Jesus. Have we not often presented a rigid system of ideas instead of an inspiration to creative thinking? There is risk involved in the latter method but there is also risk in the former; in the one the risk of freedom, in the other the risk of frustration. You cannot permit men to make their own patterns and not have some grotesque creations. On the other hand, you cannot ask men to accept in toto the mental patterns of another without a perversion of individuality and sometimes an utter inadequacy which is ruinous to personality. We, Protestants, are presumably on the side of freedom. We have always declared that only a free soul can honor God or even be a soul. We have not always understood the implications of our own position, but if it has any validity at all, it is in reference to the response of the human mind to the mind that was in Jesus. If there is a free response, there will inevitably be blundering but there will be an opportunity for fulfillments which cannot come by mere routine adherence to a pattern fixed twenty centuries ago. In one respect the Barthians are right; the word of God comes directly to the spirit of man. The teachings of Jesus may be the occasion of the birth of the Word within, but when God has a chance prepared by familiarity with the words of Jesus, God can speak directly to the human soul. Often the largest ministry of Jesus is not in any specific direction he may give in any concrete situation, but in his preparation of the soul for a new revelation which will enable it to meet its immediate problem with insight and power.

IV

Preaching that makes for personality must let people have the redemptive, liberating, unifying influence of the person of Jesus. Jules Payot, in his old but still refreshing book on *The Education of the Will,* speaks of "men who though dead are . . . more alive and more capable of transmitting life than the living." And he relates the confession of Michelet: "I remember that when the trouble came, privations of the present, fear of the future, the enemy being only two steps off, and my own enemies mocking me every day, one day . . . I gathered myself together in a huddled heap; without fire, not knowing if there would be bread to eat in the evening, as everything seemed at an end for me. . . . But I felt the virile joy of youth and the future. Who gave me this vigorous enthusiasm? Those with whom I lived my daily life; my favorite authors; I was each day drawn more closely to this noble society."[2] It is a question whether the average man can receive so much from the departed great. There is no question but that Jesus has done as much and more for men and women of all classes in society. He influences men not by teachings merely but as a teacher; not by his sayings only but by his soul; not as a mirror in which are reflected eternal values, but as a man. One of the truest things that has been written on this theme appeared recently in the *Christian Century*[3] from the pen of Professor Virgil Aldrich. The author is describing the difference between the influence of Plato and the influence of Jesus. "Men say they love Plato. They also say they love Jesus. But they really love what Plato said, the points he made, while they love Jesus himself; not the everlastingly important points he made but the everlastingly attractive person he was." That has been his unique power always, to draw men unto himself. He has made them wiser whenever they have listened to his teachings but he has made them want to be like him, to do such things as he would approve whenever they have really seen him as a living Person. When he was here, he asked men to do things for his sake. It was an audacious request. One can always ask another to do things because they are right, because they ought to be done. But not very often can one say to another, "Do it for my sake." You have to love somebody very much to have an appeal like that come home with any force. I knew a man who tried hard to do the right thing always. His life had been a struggle against often insuperable odds. He had carried on with a bravery which evoked admiration, had overcome where multitudes would have succumbed, had achieved where for multitudes there would have been only a story of failure. But there came into his life one whom he deeply loved. He told me what a change it made. He began to do things for her sake. Difficulties increased, obstacles multiplied. But the very thought of her, of her sorrow at his surrender, her glory in his triumph, spurred him on to arduous endeavor and gave him a new joy in it. There has to be a personal tie of unusual depth and intimacy ere one begins to do things "for her sake" or "for his sake." Americans revere the memory of Lincoln, but they never talk of doing things for Lincoln's sake. Englishmen are forever praising the genius of Shakespeare, but they never write for Shakespeare's sake. Frenchmen have made a lovely legend of Joan of Arc but they do not strive for Joan's sake. During the war someone wrote a song—

> "Joan of Arc, let your spirit guide us through;
> Come, lead your France to victory;
> Joan of Arc, we are calling you,"

but everybody knew that to be a mere rhapsody and not the reality that led men in and out of the trenches during four terrible years. But people do do things for Jesus' sake. A little Italian boy in Baltimore learned enough about Jesus in one of our church schools to fall in love with him and make a profession of discipleship. He was asked one day if it made any difference in his life. He answered, "One thing; it made me stop cheating in examinations." When asked why, he replied, "You can't cheat when he is looking at you." It is a far cry from Baltimore streets to the man who was picked off the Damascus road, but he felt that same constraint, "The love of Christ constraineth me." "For his sake we are counted as sheep for the slaughter." "Ourselves your servants for Jesus' sake." In every century and in every land Jesus has demonstrated that strange capacity of inspiring men to do things, of making them want to do things for his sake. The theologies with which men have described him have ranged from a trinitarianism which has been a thinly concealed tritheism to a practical unitarianism, but the response to him has been strangely unanimous; not a reaction to an idea but a truly personal response to a truly personal appeal from a truly fascinating Person. He has a unique ability when seen as a Person to become what the psychologists call "The master sentiment," so important for the unification and enrichment of personality.

Such a fact has great significance for preaching. It means that it must be the preacher's constant endeavor to let men see him, not merely his teachings but him. It demands a different kind of preaching than a mere presentation of ideas, however adequate. It is one thing to represent fairly the major emphases in a man's moral and spiritual system and another thing to so recreate the man himself that one's hearers feel that they know not only what the man taught but the man himself. There are many men who could give a fairly accurate presentation of the ideas of William Alfred Quayle, his love of nature, his love of folks, his love of God. But when Merton S. Rice speaks for two hours on "The Skylark of Methodism," one gets not a parade of ideas but a sense of the living, laughing, loving incarnation of eternal sunshine that Bishop Quayle was. He comes alive again; once again you feel the charm of his spirit, the witchery of his pulpit style, the magnificence of the man. What my friend has done for his friend, we preachers ought to do for the Friend—make him live for our congregations. He ought to be seen through every saying of his that we take as text, to be the chief impression from every sermon, the persistent presence in the pulpit, so that every time we stand there men will see behind us the historic Jesus as the sculptor has put the statue of Jesus behind that of Phillips Brooks under the eaves of Trinity Church, Boston; so that no person can listen to us even for a little while without feeling their hearts strangely warmed by the revelation of the most captivating figure in history.

That can happen only if, first of all, Jesus lives in the preacher's mind and heart. Every preacher ought to know the words of Jesus so well that if every New Testament in the world were burned, he could reconstruct in essence the Gospels out of his own memory. It is not enough to have the words of Jesus in a book on the table before us; not enough to be able to repeat the Beatitudes or the parables. All that Jesus said should exist as a living whole in the preacher's mind, so that every time he takes his pen to write or opens his mouth to speak that living unity of ideas should be informing and inspiring him. But it also means that to the preacher himself Jesus should be a living, fascinating reality. He must catch the spirit behind all the teachings, must feel the eternal charm of "manhood's best Man," must know what it is to want to do things for Jesus' sake. Then only will that voice like the voice of many waters break through all our halting speech; then only will the face which every artist has tried to capture and found elusive be seen in our pulpits; then only will that life which is the despair of all biography walk once again up and down the aisles of our churches.

V

Finally, effective preaching must reveal the unique relationship of Jesus to God. He is of value, to be sure, because of what he is in himself apart from any theories about him. There is that in him, if seen, which will always make an appeal to the human heart and become a formative influence in the pilgrimage of the self toward personality. But it is as a revelation of ultimate reality that he makes his supreme appeal. What he is in himself is captivating but, if what he is is a disclosure of what God is, then he becomes not merely a stimulus to effort but the creator of a faith that gives effort eternal significance. Doing things for Jesus' sake becomes doing things for God's sake. The sense of struggle against a hostile environment passes over into a conviction that one is laboring in harmony with something deeper, more ultimate than the immediate environment, with the final character of things. Labor becomes significant and hopeful. Just before starting for New Haven the pastor of one of our largest churches appealed to me that I should not shy away from the deity of Jesus in these lectures. I have not used that phrase at any time during this series and I cannot. It has so many confusing connotations. The eternal God was not and cannot be completely localized in any human figure. He is revealed everywhere as he is present everywhere throughout the universe, sometimes struggling with temporarily triumphant evil, sometimes appearing in triumphant good. But to me his supreme revelation came in Jesus of Nazareth. Professor Baillie wrote in *And the Life Everlasting:* "The Eternal now discloses himself to us as one who loves us with a love greater and more mysterious than our minds can comprehend, but to which the love that dwells in the heart of Christ is the most available clue."[4] That is my faith, and it is a faith which does something for preaching. Those who are contending for high views of the person of Jesus are contending for something very worth while. It does matter whether the thrilling things he says and the more thrilling things he was are merely a temporary emergence of life in the midst of a universal graveyard or are themselves a clue to the nature of Ultimate Reality. There is nothing that grips the heart so inescapably and stimulates the mind so persistently as a conviction that what Jesus was God is, and that our struggle to be like him has the universe as an ally, and that our striving selves in the effort to achieve personality are not mere "valiant dust that builds on dust" but co-laborers with God. If the Ideal Person is also the clue to the character of the Eternal Person, then there is hope that we all may become persons, in a fellowship of persons which includes God, and the pilgrims of an eternal progress.

REFERENCES

Chapter Two

1, 2, 3, 4. *Zion's Herald,* November 22, 1933.

5. *The Great Offensive,* p. 326. Maurice Hindus. Harrison Smith and Robert Haas. By permission.

6. *Personality and Social Adjustment,* p. 13. Ernest R. Groves. Longmans, Green & Co., publishers. By permission.

7. *What Is Salvation?* p. 164. E. S. Waterhouse. Cokesbury Press.

8. *Personality and Social Adjustment,* p. 246. Ernest R. Groves. By permission.

9. *Psycho-Analysis for Normal People,* p. 137. Geraldine Coster. Oxford University Press.

10. *The Inner World of Childhood,* p. 132. Frances G. Wickes. D. Appleton-Century Company. By permission.

11. *A Psychological Approach to Theology,* p. 135. Walter M. Horton. Harper & Brothers, publishers. By permission.

Chapter Three

1. *Mens Creatrix,* p. 126. William Temple. The Macmillan Company.

2. *The Significance of Personality,* p. 27. Richard M. Vaughn. By permission of The Macmillan Company, publishers.

3. *Living Philosophies,* p. 130. Simon & Schuster, Inc. By permission.

4. *Atlantic Monthly Magazine,* January, 1934. Grace Adams.

5. *The Motives of Men,* p. 145. George A. Coe. Charles Scribner's Sons.

6, 7. *Studies in Sublime Failure,* p. 61. Ernest Benn, Ltd., London.

8. "Nancy Hanks." Rosemary Benét. Copyright, 1933, by Rosemary and Vincent Benét. Published by Farrar & Rinehart. Reprinted by permission of the authors.

9. *Studies in Sublime Failure.* Shane Leslie. Ernest Benn, Ltd., London.

10. Rudyard Kipling. By permission of author. Watt & Son, publishers, London, and Doubleday, Doran and Company.

Chapter Four

1. *The Normal Mind,* p. 537. William H. Burnham. D. Appleton-Century Company.

2. *Living Philosophies,* p. 29. Simon & Schuster. By permission.

3. *Harper's Magazine,* January, 1934, "How Not to Write History."

4. *The Gospel and Its Tributaries,* pp. 51 and 52. Ernest F. Scott. T. & T. Clark, Edinburgh.

5, 6. *The Life of Jesus,* p. 215. Maurice Goguel. By permission of The Macmillan Company, publishers.

7, 8, 9, 10. *The Psychic Health of Jesus,* pp. 250, 253, 268. Walter E. Bundy. By permission of The Macmillan Company, publishers.

11. *The Life of Jesus,* p. 389. Maurice Goguel. By permission of The Macmillan Company, publishers.

12. "Lighten Our Darkness," Studdert-Kennedy, quoted in *Religious Experience the Methodist Fundamental.* Holborn Publishing House.

13. *The Lord of Thought,* p. 224. Dougall & Emmett.

14. Quoted in *The Finality of Jesus Christ,* p. 211. R. E. Speer.

15. In paper written for the Delaware Conference on "The Significance of Jesus Christ."

16. "The Stormers of Heaven," Freehof, quoted in *The Finality of Jesus Christ,* p. 211. R. E. Speer.

Chapter Five

1. *The Doctor Looks at Love and Life.* Joseph Collins. Copyright, 1926, by Doubleday, Doran and Company, Inc. By permission.

2. *The Normal Mind,* p. 473. W. H. Burnham. D. Appleton-Century Company, publishers. By permission.

3. "The Refuge of the Impersonal." *Atlantic Monthly Magazine,* January, 1934.

4, 5. *The Problem of Conduct,* pp. 257, 259. A. E. Taylor. By permission of The Macmillan Company, publishers.

6. *Studies in Sublime Failure,* in loc. Shane Leslie.

7. *Power,* p. 437. Lion Feuchtwanger. Copyright, 1926, by the Viking Press, Inc., New York.

8. *What I Owe to Christ,* p. 209. C. F. Andrews. The Abingdon Press.

9. *The Person of Christ,* p. 178. L. W. Grensted. Harper & Brothers, publishers. By permission.

10. *The Person of Christ,* p. 161. L. W. Grensted. Harper & Brothers, publishers. By permission.

11. *Contemporary American Philosophy,* p. 109. George P. Adams and William P. Montague. By permission of The Macmillan Company, publishers.

CHAPTER SIX

1. *The Inner World of Childhood,* p. 221. Frances B. Wickes. D. Appleton-Century Company. By permission.

2. *Psycho-Analysis for Normal People,* p. 139. Geraldine Coster. Oxford University Press.

3. *The Ivory Door,* p. 65. A. A. Milne. Samuel French & Co. By permission.

4. *The Ivory Door,* p. 57. A. A. Milne. Samuel French & Co. By permission.

5. *Studies in Sublime Failure.* Shane Leslie.

CHAPTER SEVEN

1. *Mens Creatrix,* p. 111. William Temple. The Macmillan Company.

2. *The Rebellious Puritan,* p. 113. Lloyd Morris. Harcourt, Brace & Company, publishers. By permission.

3. *Sonnets From the Portuguese.* Mrs. Browning.

4. *The Psychological Approach to Theology,* p. 126. Walter M. Horton. Harper & Brothers, publishers. By permission.

5. *The Ivory Door,* p. 67. A. A. Milne. Samuel French & Co. By permission.

6. *Sonnets From the Portuguese.* Mrs. Browning.

7. *Property, Its Duties and Rights,* p. 197. By permission of The Macmillan Company, publishers.

CHAPTER EIGHT

1. *An Introduction to the Psychology of Religion,* p. 54. R. H. Thouless. By permission of The Macmillan Company, publishers.

2. *The Religious Consciousness,* p. 145. James Bissett Pratt. By permission of The Macmillan Company, publishers.

3. *The Quest of the Historical Jesus,* p. 401. A. Schweitzer.

4. *An Introduction to the Psychology of Religion,* p. 55. R. H. Thouless. By permission of The Macmillan Company, publishers.

5. *The Life of Jesus,* p. 560. Maurice Goguel. By permission of The Macmillan Company, publishers.

6. *The Christian Experience of Forgiveness,* p. 190. H. R. Mackintosh. Harper & Brothers, publishers. By permission.

7. *Peter Abelard,* p. 181. Helen Waddell. Henry Holt and Company. By permission.

8. *Peter Abelard,* p. 28. Helen Waddell. Henry Holt and Company. By permission.

CHAPTER NINE

1. *I Follow the Road.* Anne Byrd Payson. The Abingdon Press.

2. *The Education of the Will,* p. 412. Jules Payot. Funk & Wagnalls Company. By permission.

3. *Christian Century.*

4. *And the Life Everlasting,* p. 194. John Baillie. Charles Scribner's Sons, publishers. By permission.